Make Lasting Changes:
The Science of Sustainable Behavior Change and Reaching Your Goals

By Peter Hollins

Author and Researcher at

petehollins.com

Table of Contents

Make Lasting Changes: The Science of Sustainable Behavior Change and Reaching Your Goals 3
Table of Contents 5
Introduction 7
Chapter 1. Models of Behavior Change 13
Chapter 2. What's Holding You Back? 41
Chapter 3. What's Pushing You Forward? ... 61
Chapter 4. Start Your Engines 77
Chapter 5. Maintain Momentum 103
Chapter 6. Correcting Course 123
Chapter 7. Environment 147
Chapter 8. Building Lasting Habits 165
Chapter 9. Design Flaws 179
Summary Guide 189

Introduction

One of my favorite television shows used to be *The Biggest Loser*. If you are unfamiliar with it, the premise is overweight or obese people are given personal trainers and nutritionists and told to lose as much weight as possible.

It's a competition where the winner receives some life-changing amount of money, so you can imagine that people are quite motivated to change their behavior as much as possible. Many dramatic tears are shed along the way, and there is no shortage of inspirational montages.

These days, I'm more impatient, so I only tune into the last few episodes, where you can see some incredible transformations. People tend to cut their body weight in half, and they appear to lose ages of wear and tear along with the weight. Some of them look like legitimate supermodels after they've reached their goal weights.

However, after the show ends, almost without fail, most of the contestants revert back to their original body weight. Some even gain weight after the fact. We're talking about regaining 200 pounds that were shed after a huge amount of sweat and tears. Objectively speaking, it's actually a challenge to gain that much weight. You'd almost have to be deliberately trying.

So why does this happen? Why don't the contestants from the television show make lasting changes, and why are their results always so short-lived?

There are many: loss of environments tailor-made for them, loss of trainers, loss of nutritionists, loss of rewards dangling in front of them, loss of sources of motivation, loss of peers to commiserate with, and loss of social pressures of being on television. These are all aspects of how we can lose our willpower, self-discipline, and sense of purpose. Remove one of these legs and the whole thing might come crumbling down.

Changing your behavior to make lasting changes is a complex maze of dealing with our fickle and compulsive minds. We may know logically and intellectually what we must do, but most of the time, that simply doesn't matter. We can have the best intentions in the world, but so what? We might even have the weight of the world hanging over us, but that doesn't always matter, either.

We can start with motivation, but motivation tends to be temporary and is a short-term solution. Habits are important, but they can take at least a few weeks to really form. What about dealing with fears, failure, and insecurities? No matter how irrational some are, others are grounded in some version of reality and can be paralyzing.

Though much of making lasting changes is grounded in experimentation, the most obvious being Pavlov's experiments with his dog, it is more of an art than a science because everyone has different values and interests. For each person, you have to adjust each knob and dial to just the right amount to create an unstoppable, motivated, change-making machine. Like Kentucky Fried Chicken's secret blend of herbs and spices, everyone has a combination of factors that works but has to be discovered through good ol' testing.

Maybe the pitfall of the contestants on *The Biggest Loser* was that they were mainly motivated by the monetary reward, and when that was removed, the other factors didn't prove strong enough to maintain a change. Whatever the case, it is clear that most did not discover their prime combination of factors.

The intention of this book is to educate and arm you with all of the factors that influence making changes to your own behavior, and also show what your secret blend will be. It may not be what you think it currently is, and I can tell you from personal experience that it probably won't be something logical!

Chapter 1. Models of Behavior Change

"You can't teach an old dog new tricks," the cliché goes. Many of us believe humans are so established in their thoughts, feelings, and habits that trying to alter our behavior is a chancy prospect at best, foolish at worst.

One might think behavior is so ingrained in us that we'd be going against nature in trying to change it. Even if we know certain attitudes and actions are holding us back or causing harm, modifying them might seem too daunting a task, resulting in our feeling hopeless and resigned. And to be honest, some behavior is indeed so deeply ingrained that we probably won't be able to change it without intensive therapy or amnesia. And before you write yourself off, that's only true in 1% of cases, and it likely does not apply to you.

Change isn't easy or even pleasurable at times, but it's important. The rewards we open ourselves up to as the result of change are well worth the emotional expenses of fear, trepidation, and anxiety we spend going through it. Anything we want in life, we will have to engage in a journey to attain. A journey has a beginning point and an end point—change is the only constant in life.

But what does it *mean to* change our behavior?

You might consider it to be transforming or eliminating certain habits, actions, and thoughts that are reliably there and therefore consistent. They make us comfortable because they are familiar and represent a certain sort of safety—even if they make us miserable. Or you might think it's self-development, consciousness-raising and awareness, or skill-building in order to attain a goal.

Behavior change encompasses all those aspects in one way or another. But that's on the shallow level; there is a far deeper level how changing your behaviors affects you mentally and emotionally. It's a sweeping reworking of our very foundation: how we learn, how we enhance ourselves, how we execute on our drive and motives, and how we distinguish ourselves from others. It's a full program designed to help us live the life we want, more fully and assuredly. Quite simply, it's how we learn to appreciate and be happy with ourselves and to get the kind of existence we want.

Certainly, much of the foundation for our personal satisfaction is a matter of perspective. There's something to be said for attitude adjustment and accepting what we can in our lives. But true behavioral change covers both our viewpoint *and* our surroundings. Refiguring our mindset is the beginning of the process; the end game is transformation of our circumstances.

That kind of active change is the point of this book. The old dog isn't unable to learn new tricks—he's just stubborn and people have given up on him because he's old. He also can't read. But you can. So we'll concentrate on you.

Historical Models of Behavioral Change

As long as psychiatry has existed, its golden objective has been effecting permanent changes in mental processes to achieve a desirable outcome. It has long been understood that this is a process that begins from the inside out, and as you can imagine, several different models of behavioral improvement have been floated throughout the centuries, each with its own focus and philosophy. To frame your own journey to making lasting changes, it is helpful to review them to understand the basis of the tools you might be using.

Classical conditioning. As the name implies, classical conditioning is the most famous kind of behavioral change, typified by the almost folkloric experiments of Russian physiologist Ivan Pavlov in the 1900s.

Pavlov noticed (don't ask why he was paying attention) that his dogs salivated whenever he entered the room. Figuring that the dog's response had something to do with the fact that he was its food source, Pavlov set up some trials with his canine friends. In the first stage, he rang a bell when he presented the dogs their meals. After a few repetitions, he then simply rang the bell but didn't bring the meals. Pavlov found his dogs still salivated at the sound of the bell, even if there was no food accompanying it.

In this experiment, the food is what we call the *natural stimulus*: that's specifically what the dogs were looking forward to and made them drool. The bell Pavlov rang at mealtime was a *neutral stimulus*. Before the experiments, the dogs wouldn't have reacted to the sound of the bell by salivating. But after they came to associate it so closely with their feeding schedule, the bell by itself was cause for the dogs to start their slobbering, whether or not it came with food.

This is the heart of classical conditioning: forming a reflexive action by pairing a natural stimulus with a neutral one. You're conditioned to respond because you've now formed a mental connection between two items, which allows you to evoke at will the type of behavior or action you want.

For example, say you had a difficult time in a history class in high school. Maybe the teacher had a crusade against you, or you flunked every test, or some of the better students in the class taunted you. Whatever happened, it was at least mildly traumatic. Years later, you might find yourself getting anxious, flustered, or nauseous at the sight of a history book. If you'd had a neutral or positive experience in history class, you wouldn't have such an adverse reaction to the book.

That's classical conditioning at work, albeit unintentionally, which is how it most frequently occurs in our lives. But you can deliberately use the tenets of this theory to effect behavior change by finding more positive stimulus pairings or eliminating negative ones.

Operant conditioning. A few years later, behavioral psychologist B.F. Skinner sought to amplify (if not repudiate) the effects of classical conditioning with something less simplistic. Skinner's views were supported by his experiments with positive and negative *reinforcement* of certain behaviors.

Skinner experimented on rats. He put them in boxes, each of which had an empty food bowl and a lever attached to the sides. As the rat moved about the box, it would inadvertently knock into the lever—which then caused a food pellet to drop into the trough. The rat then ate the food. Pretty quickly, the rat realized that hitting the lever produced food—a *positive* reinforcement. The rat knew anytime it wanted food, it just had to work that lever. So it did, again and again. The rat was thus conditioned into a specific behavior on the basis of wanting a reward.

On the other hand, Skinner also probed the effects of *negative* reinforcement. In these trials, he put the rats in boxes, each of which again had levers on the walls. But it also had electric currents running across the floor, which caused unpleasant shocks to the rat. In panicked attempts to escape the rat would, again accidentally, run into the lever, which switched off the electric current. In time, the rat learned that whenever it was put into a box, the first thing it needed to do was depress that lever to prevent itself from being shocked.

This system of shaping behavior is called operant conditioning. If a subject displays the desired behavior, then they are compensated with a reward. If the subject *doesn't* display the behavior, they're punished. After the learning phase, the subjects have lasting behavior changes as a result of subconsciously anticipating the reward or punishment.

For example, a teacher subtly bribes children who clean up their workspaces with gold stars and candy. The teacher doesn't give any of these to a child who does not clean up their workspace—a negative reinforcement. Quickly, the children develop the habit of cleaning their workspaces because of the pending delivery of candy and gold stars. Soon thereafter, the children clean their workspaces even if candy and gold stars aren't promised because they are subconsciously anticipating them.

Operant conditioning also works by subtraction. If a subject shows the wanted behavior, the controller could *take away* a certain negative thing from the subject. Likewise, if they show an undesirable behavior, they could take something positive away as a punishment or negative reinforcement.

The big difference from the classical method is that operant conditioning focuses on *voluntary* actions, not reflexive ones. Pavlov's dogs couldn't help salivating, but Skinner's rats actively made the *choice* to pull the levers. This makes it easy to self-motivate: if you're working to make a change and do something positive, remember to give yourself some sort of prize. Even a small one can give you the reinforcement you need.

Tiny habits. Stanford psychology professor B.J. Fogg, whose main focus is the power of persuasion, believes the key to behavior change is starting on a much smaller scale than one might think is necessary. Fogg's research established, according to his website, that "only three things will change behavior in the long term":

- Have an epiphany: "My friend was killed in a drunk driving accident, so I want to be sober now."

- Change your context: "I moved apartments so I am now next door to the gym; I now have no choice but to go every day."

- Take baby steps: "If I just floss one tooth today, I can floss two tomorrow."

Generally speaking, we can't control when we get sudden bursts of knowledge or revelation, so Fogg dismisses epiphanies as part of a program and prefers to focus on the latter two. But changing one's environment and making minor but consistent adjustments to routines are steps that we *can* execute ourselves.

To that end, Fogg has developed a successful and intriguing method for behavior change called "tiny habits." The concept is very uncomplicated: introduce a very brief routine—no more than 30 seconds—over the course of a given period of time.

Fogg cites incorporating dental floss as one of his favorite examples. After brushing your teeth, start flossing just *one* tooth. The next time you brush your teeth, floss *two* teeth. The time after that, floss *three* teeth. As you develop this habit gradually, at the end of 32 days you'll be flossing each and every chomper you have in your mouth.

The "tiny habits" theory can be applied to a surprisingly wide range of behaviors. For example, to work on "love" habits, Fogg suggests small changes of expression: "After I walk in the door from work, I will kiss my spouse" or "After I change my baby's diaper, I will give her a hug."

In business, when a colleague completes a task you needed, you can start thanking them in person rather than by email. If you're trying to incorporate a new exercise into your daily routine, start with three reps for the first time, move on to six, and so on.

Fogg's point is that it's easier and far more practical to incorporate new habits on a gradual basis rather than creating grand expectations and trying to overhaul your routine all at once.

Cognitive behavioral therapy. The above three methods approach change from a perspective of action—they deal with things that you do. But in the 1960s, psychiatrist Aaron Beck developed a method that sought to change how we think about and perceive things.

During his psychoanalysis sessions with patients, Beck noticed that many of them were conducting internal dialogues with themselves. Many of these inner discussions took the shape of emotionally charged "automatic thoughts" in which the patients frequently belittled themselves or distorted the truth about harmless events. But they were so brief that the patients—who may have been mostly unaware of them—only reported fragments of these dialogues back to Beck.

Beck's goal was to help his subjects recognize those thoughts as they were happening, as he believed that detecting them was an important step in his clients' dealing with their problems. He called his method "cognitive therapy" to reflect that it was a mental process: patients had to concentrate on their thoughts to effectuate change.

Over time the method became known as "cognitive behavioral therapy" (CBT), as it's come to incorporate behavioral tactics along with mental ones. Several types of therapies now fall under this banner, and the parts of each method differ somewhat from the next. But CBT has proven to be successful in scientific experiments across a broad scope of teams and patients, and it has been employed to solve a large range of issues. It may not be used by all psychologists, but it is used by most to some degree or another.

Instead of examining events in the distant past like traditional psychoanalysis does, CBT patients concentrate on what's happening *now* and what they are thinking *now*. They explore their current thoughts, feelings, and actions to test how they contribute to a certain problem. Then they zero in on practical solutions to change ways of thinking and eliminate destructive habits.

For example, a college student finishes a term paper, which his professor reviews with him personally. The professor compliments the student's way with words, his command of allegories, and his keen insights—but also offers constructive criticism that he could use a little editing to say more with less. The student ignores all the positive remarks his teacher had and focuses only on the last, only slightly negative remark about his editing. He then allows that one singular comment to fuel feelings of disappointment and hopelessness—completely overlooking the many fine points of his paper that the teacher described. This is an example of an automatic thought pattern that needs to change.

If that student underwent CBT, his analyst might pinpoint his inclination to dwell only on the (only moderately) negative feedback his professor offered and ignore his very encouraging statements. It would be discovered that the student has low self-confidence and suffers from massive imposter syndrome. Hopefully, the analyst would be able to help the student acknowledge that habit and take a more reasonable view of the encounter and others like it. CBT fosters a patient's stepping outside their mental or emotional reflexes, observing them in an objective light, and learning how to adjust their internal behaviors to alleviate their difficulties.

Six Stages of Behavior Change

Of all the models that we've considered for the purpose of changing behavior, one stood out as the most detailed and all-inclusive. It's also the one that's most suited for application in our everyday lives and reflects much of what we'll talk about later in this book. Practitioners call it the *transtheoretical model of change* (or the "readiness-to-change" model), but for the purposes of this book, we'll just refer to it as the six stages of behavior change.

The method was developed by James O. Prochaska, Ph.D., in the early '80s. Its basic premise is that making a change, no matter how much it's desired, doesn't happen just because we make one single decision to do so. It's the result of a progression that includes thoughts, deliberation, taking tentative steps, making mistakes, and sometimes even failing (but starting over). Indeed, this proposal reflects real life: just because we make a decision to eat healthily doesn't mean we can suddenly overcome temptations and make the right food choices.

Prochaska identified the six stages of complete and meaningful behavior changes as follows—and they're essentially what the chapters following this one will outline in greater detail. For purposes of explanation, we'll use the very common example of quitting drinking to illustrate these phases.

1. Precontemplation. The first stage in behavioral change is, paradoxically, not thinking you need to change.

There might be any one of several reasons we're not ready to make a specific change: we don't have the time or the energy, we've tried before and failed, or we just don't think the advantages the change might bring about are worth the effort.

One is likely to know that there's a change they *should* make but regard it as something they'll do down the road, at some certain point, only when an impossible list of pre-requirements has been met. They don't consider it a pressing need. Consequently, they cut off or dismiss all discussions and thoughts about it and delay its onset even longer.

In our example, the precontemplation phase for a problem drinker is simply a state of denial: they don't think they have a problem. The characteristics of an alcoholic don't apply to them. Alternately, they may have just accepted that they're always going to be an alcoholic, that any attempt to change will fail, and the end result wouldn't be worth the effort they have to make.

This stage is important because it allows people to continue in the destructive behavior they want to continue, and it sets the stage for crashing, burning, and generally realizing that change is actually necessary for greater happiness.

2. Contemplation. At this stage, you've perhaps realized that change might be necessary. You're sick of suffering or feeling hungover all the time. You're starting to consider it as a preferred course of action, but nothing too urgent. You may have considered that you'll make the transformation over a long, or future, period of time—but you won't be starting terribly soon.

Unlike the precontemplation phase, you're more open to receiving information about the change. You might begin asking others who have already made the transformation about their experiences. You'll start a reasonable analysis of what kind of effect changing will have on you, using various sources and perspectives to do so. You might start to plan, but it's the type of planning that is essentially procrastination.

When the contemplator assesses all this information and starts investigating their *own* motivations and how the change will affect them personally, then the watershed moment of decision becomes imminent. How strongly do you want to make this change? What do you need to do, and how will it affect your daily life? Those questions could be the precursor to the next step.

For our problem drinker, a cataclysmic event may have woken them up a little and made them realize they might have an issue. They might have wrecked a car while driving drunk or damaged or ended a close relationship because of abusive behavior while intoxicated. Although they're not ready to commit and still uncertain of their abilities, they're now taking the idea somewhat seriously.

3. Preparation. At this point, you've established that you want to take action. The benefits of changing surpass the disadvantages, and your question has been answered at least philosophically.

But you're not quite ready to go all in; you have to build up your reserve of confidence first. You have to make a lot of devoted consideration about what you're about to do. You strategize about the steps, you make outlines or plans for your process, and you try to evaluate what obstacles or challenges might emerge and how you'll handle them. Frankly, you're scared of failing, change, and the associated struggle of change.

Preparation can take a while, and people tend to stay in this phase a bit longer than necessary as a means of procrastination, yet again. You're gathering information and setting up avenues of personal support. You might (and should) be setting up a schedule of milestones you want to hit on your journey and building a help network. You could even be buying supplies if needed. You're finishing up a detailed blueprint that will guide you through the change.

At this point, the problem drinker has realized they have to do something, so they start making small arrangements. They may have started looking for AA or other rehab-oriented meetings and finding a sponsor, or they have begun seeing a personal counselor. They might have thrown out all the liquor in their house. They're planning their recovery.

4. Action. Now it's game time: you have begun your program to change. You're not just thinking about it. You have stopped a behavior you don't want and have started ones you do.

But you're still very susceptible to reverting back to your old ways—which is why this stage is *not* necessarily the time to focus on goals or achievement. Rather, this is when you concentrate solely on progress and accumulate confidence. You seek ongoing support from others, you chart your development, and you replace your old environments and actions with new, healthful ones.

You'll also likely be caught in this stage for a long time—however many days, weeks, or even months it will take you to fully absorb your new behavior and integrate it in as many parts of your life as possible. Unlike the previous stages, Prochaska gives the action phase a fairly precise time of six months. He estimated it would take a staggering six months of active, painful work to alter a routine and behavior. No wonder people procrastinate.

The problem drinker in our example has now stopped drinking. They're participating in meetings (or at least going regularly), discussing their problems with counselors or friends, and keeping track of their daily process. They're finding ways to hold themselves accountable and possibly even talking to others who are just starting their journey to recovery. They understand intellectually and logically why they must stop, and they are working toward controlling their urges. Most importantly, they're taking it day by day.

5. Maintenance. After six months of action, Prochaska says, you've fully merged your behavioral change into your lifestyle. You've overcome the barriers, beaten temptation, and built up your confidence. The change you once believed was a remote and difficult prospect is now a fully realized aspect of your life. You feel that you have full control most of the time.

However, even though the risk of relapse has been greatly reduced, it's not completely absent. A quick instance of going back to your old habit can send you back in the opposite direction. A major life event, especially a catastrophic one like divorce or death of a family member, can restart the destructive behavior you've just changed.

Part of maintenance mode is dealing with those prospects and proactively strengthening yourself to cope with these potential triggers. It's building up new sources of personal power and renewing your accomplishment so that it continues to help you improve. Prochaska also gives a general time frame for the maintenance stage: two years.

Our problem drinker is considerably healthier at this point. Their newfound sobriety makes up the center of their personality, and they may have overcome the most difficult part of their rehabilitation. But they know their past life isn't that far behind them yet. They may have occasional temptations to drink or feel overly secure that they can now *handle* one drink or two. Hopefully, they'll keep reminding themselves how easy it would be to fall back into old patterns—they're just one drink away from reversing their change. They've shown great improvement but haven't stopped being self-vigilant.

6. Termination. The final stage is when the change you wanted to make is no longer a "change"—it's done. It's now a permanent part of who you are. You no longer feel the lure of your old habits. You might not even think of them anymore. Prochaska says only about 15–20% of people on this six-stage journey make it to termination phase. In truth, that feels like a high estimate.

But the termination stage isn't just when you sit still and rest on your laurels. You might be inspired and more able to take on new challenges that build upon the change that you've made. At this point, having achieved your one major goal of change, other goals that might have seemed impossible before are now completely feasible. So for many, the termination part is a springboard to new opportunities that you're now far more able to accept.

For all intents and purposes, our problem drinker has now ceased to exist, because drinking is no longer a problem for them. Alcohol isn't a part of their life in any way, because the temptation to drink isn't there and hasn't been for a long time. Furthermore, now they're ready to take advantage of new experiences and chances that once seemed utterly out of the question because alcohol was standing in their way.

Behavior change is not a cakewalk—especially when even *admitting* we need to change is hard to do. So the first part of any long-term effort to transform our behavior can be tricky but is absolutely crucial. How do we determine what the problem really is and what stands in the way of our solving it? Let's find out.

Takeaways:

- Behavior change is not a new topic, as people have wanted to improve themselves for millennia. The more recent, historical models of behavior change inform the framework for what we use today.

- Historical models of behavior change include classical conditioning (unconscious association), operant conditioning (trained actions), tiny habits (taking baby steps, changing your context, or having an epiphany), and cognitive behavioral theory (fixing automatic thought patterns that are detrimental).

- The transtheoretical model of change is what parallels daily struggle the most thoroughly and is composed of six stages: precontemplation, contemplation, preparation, action, maintenance, and termination.

Chapter 2. What's Holding You Back?

For the most part, nobody questions why behavioral change is necessary.

Most people can immediately list the benefits of having a healthy diet, exercising, quitting smoking, improving relationship communication, or any other positive personal adjustments we can make. And those who can't answer can find out easily from family, friends, and the more reputable sites on the Internet. We know, logically, why change is good. We know staying the course is detrimental and has a host of negative consequences. We know staying still is the same as continuing on the harmful path.

So why don't we do it?

Well, it's always easier said than done. It's one thing to understand from an intellectual standpoint; it's quite another to put it into action. Knowing doesn't replace doing. But why isn't just *knowing* why we should do something enough to *motivate* us?

As wonderful a tool as the brain is, in fact we're driven by a lot of factors that have little to do with logic. In fact, you can argue that logic is far, far down on the list of factors that influence our daily actions. Evolutionarily, this means logic probably wasn't a big reason our species survived. We may have the inspiration, sustained interest, and determination—but there are other forces, both internal and external, that keep us from effecting meaningful change.

It's now well documented how harmful smoking can be to one's health. The science is long-established and fairly ironclad. Nobody will tell you smoking's good for you, not even cigarette manufacturers, who are legally required to tell you that it contributes to death and various ailments. But many can't quit because their addiction to nicotine is too strong, and they fear the physical feelings of withdrawal that will come if they stop smoking. Their logical brains know the benefits; their illogical bodies couldn't care less. Their illogical bodies just want to seek pleasure and to avoid pain.

These illogical obstacles to behavior change come from many directions, so it's helpful to organize them into three realms: *conscious, subconscious, and external factors*. The reason these three categories were chosen is that they accurately represent our thought processes in daily life. We are conscious of our own limitations, we don't realize all of our own limitations, and sometimes we can't help but fall prey to an outside limitation.

Conscious Psychological Factors

Some of our negative reactions to the idea of changing come from places we're well aware of. They're preexistent problems we consciously know we have. They're attitudes about ourselves that, given a little prodding, we might readily admit we possess. Although overcoming these self-thoughts are difficult, it's not impossible. In fact, they're far easier to diagnose and treat than the subconscious factors we'll cover in a few minutes. But our conscious obstructions are equally as important to watch and hopefully reduce as much as possible.

Low self-esteem and confidence. *"I just can't do it. I'm not strong or disciplined enough."*

Maybe the most common internal factor is the feeling that we just can't do it. We're not good, strong, smart, or agile enough to get it done. Often we compare ourselves to other people who seem to do what we want to do quite easily, and we know we'll never measure up to their abilities. We'll never be as good as that actor, that singer, that motivational speaker, that politician, or even that friend of ours that seems to handle everything beautifully. We make all these unfair comparisons, while we forget that at one time their level of expertise was exactly what ours is now—not much.

Negative self-image. *"I'm just not the type of person to do this. I never will be."*

This is similar to low self-esteem but may be even more destructive and tragic. More than just feeling that we can't do something, negative self-image is thinking that we don't even *deserve* to. All possibilities of change and action are closed to us because we're not worthy. This strain of thought is more dangerous than low self-esteem because it implies that we're condemned to an unfulfilling life, so even just attempting to change ourselves is a waste of time. A person with low self-esteem might still believe they're at least *entitled* to a better existence, but someone with a negative self-image doesn't believe they merit any kind of positivity at all: "I don't deserve a happy relationship because I've been doomed all my life" or "I don't deserve to be successful at work—that level of prosperity is only for people better than me."

Over-tolerance of pain or discomfort. *"I might be coughing all the time from smoking too much, but the withdrawal would be way worse."*

Endurance and strength during times of hardship are good traits, but if unchecked they can obscure realities about our situations. If we suffer injury, tribulation, or distress merely because we have faith that things will eventually get better, we could be promoting inaction. The current situation might be awful, but trying to do something about it might make it even worse. So nothing is done—and nothing changes. This can also be disguised as simple denial and denying that the pain is intense to avoid taking action.

Confrontation avoidance. *"I don't know. I don't want to upset them and make it awkward."*

The act of change almost inevitably entails some sort of conflict. Certainly you'll experience tension with yourself, against some of your oldest and ugliest truths. But you might also clash with other people who aren't tuned in to the change you're undergoing or who might be opposed or uncooperative about it. Rather than deal with these kinds of confrontations in a constructive way, one might be more inclined to retreat into a familiar bubble and avoid the possibility of facing the consequences: "This yoga class might make my ultra-religious mother upset."

Fear of failure or rejection. *"Everyone's going to laugh at my painting anyway, so I'm not going to take that art class."*

Every single attempt to bring about change runs the risk of disappointment. But for some, the possibility of failure is a terrifying concept: it reinforces their worst fears about their abilities or lack thereof and drives them to the belief that they're better off not even trying. Similarly, the often-exaggerated fear of being dismissed or criticized by other people can immobilize one's efforts to change. They might, therefore, reject the proposed change preemptively—before they suffer rejection themselves. Their current level of suffering is a walk in the park compared to confirming how incapable or untalented they are.

Subconscious Psychological Factors

If they're not immediately recognizable, conscious attitudes are at least well known enough that we can ultimately identify them somewhat quickly. Not so with subconscious factors.

These forces operate without our knowledge; we don't perceive that they're having a negative effect on our drive to change (or even just exist). They are extremely potent at eroding our self-attitudes and often recur in our lives over a very long period of time, to the extent that they derail our entire life story. These are the automatic negative thoughts and beliefs that cognitive behavioral therapy seeks to exorcise.

Many of these subconscious factors share common points with the conscious ones we've just discussed. But the subconscious factors can be more dangerous because they've been chipping away at our identities relatively undetected—and are therefore more strongly woven into our beings. They're working on us under the total cover of darkness, so it's harder to call them up and deal with them head-on.

Limiting beliefs and narratives. *"Impossible for me. I've never been that type of person."*

These are similar to the conscious negativity generated by low self-esteem and poor self-image—but they get started when we're young and become part of ourselves without our knowing. You are locked into a narrow view of what you can do or what's *proper* for you to do. You see life through a lens of pessimism and doubt. You mistrust good fortune or positivity. You're obsessed with catastrophe and dismissive of happiness.

And if a certain story doesn't fit into your oppositional point of view, you'll *make* it fit: "I'm not going for that promotion because that level of success turns people into jerks" or "Falling in love and intimacy are overrated, inconvenient, and usually very expensive—I got no time for that." This is the story you keep telling yourself, about yourself, couched in negative undertones. You've done it for so long it is a part of your identity, for better or worse. You literally cannot think in a different manner, and your worldview is skewed in a very unique way.

Fixed mindset. *"It's just not something I'll ever improve at. I'm destined to be bad forever."*

This is a twist on the self-identity factors, originally introduced by Stanford psychologist Carol Dweck. The fixed mindset declares that the traits we have are permanent and unchangeable. Our intelligence, temperament, personality, and creative talent cannot be significantly altered. Therefore, the fixed mindset defines success as how well those traits stack up against those of others, usually in a quantitative way. Since those traits can never be altered or improved in a fixed mindset, triumph is only seen as a way to prove how big those traits are. Failure is therefore dreadfully feared, as it's only perceived by the fixed mindset as evidence that we're stupid, untalented, or lacking in character—things that can't be changed.

"Growth mindsets," though, are oriented toward the tenet that all those traits are malleable and can always be improved upon: you *can* increase your intelligence, you *can* learn a talent, you *can* make adjustments to your personality. Therefore, the growth mindset embraces challenges, seeing failure as a learning opportunity and a pivot toward expanding ourselves—*not* proof of unintelligence or inability.

These mindsets can be implanted in us at a critically young age, and they hold the keys to our behaviors and attitudes toward success and failure in everything, professionally and personally speaking. They therefore have a direct impact on our faculties for satisfaction and happiness.

A fixed mindset would say, "This job requires things I'm terrible at and will never get better at," whereas a growth mindset would say, "This job looks challenging—*and I can't wait to get started on it!*"

Past experience or trauma. *"I don't know. It went terribly once before so it probably will again this time."*

What we've gone through in the past has an ongoing and direct impact on how we approach or elude certain situations later in life (similar to the classical and operant conditioning we discussed in the first chapter). While that may seem like an obvious statement few would disagree with, in practice the influence happens without our discerning.

Most of our responses to such stimuli—indeed, the stimuli itself—stem from our subconscious. We don't understand why we have such aversion or disgust toward certain things or what led to those negative feelings in the first place. It then follows quite easily into our refusing to change our existent behavior or shunning unfamiliar ones. Someone might be scared of romantic commitments because their parents seemed terminally unhappy or abusive to each other. They might not want to learn to drive because they were part of a car wreck as a child.

External Environmental Factors

This third plank of avoidance in changing behavior is significant enough that it deserves its own chapter—so I'll give it one later in this book. But I'm also briefly mentioning them here because these environmental barriers "work" side by side with the internal forces preventing us from changing our behaviors. It is notable to mention that some of these are legitimate, while others are rationalizations to avoid taking action.

Lack of practical knowledge or education. *"I don't even know what I don't know."*

Simply put, you don't have (or don't think you have) sufficient instruction, training, or information to pursue the change you want. Alternately, you can't find any way to get that kind of knowledge, even in the age of super-information. "I can't even boil water—how am I going to learn how to cook Indian food?" "I can't afford that transcendental meditation class, so I might as well forget about it."

Of course, information has never been easier to find—if anything, there is too much information available, which would cause analysis paralysis. Yet still, some people don't know where to start.

Too many obligations. *"I'm way too busy for that. I work and have seven kids and eight dogs."*

Adult responsibilities have this way of piling up to the point of overload: family, partners, children, work, home maintenance, car maintenance, bills—take your pick. This not only affects your schedule for working on change, but also could just drain you so much that you're not even aware of the changes you need to make. "Yeah, between driving the kids to school and soccer class, finishing this work project, getting the roof gutter fixed, remembering my sister's birthday, and cleaning out the refrigerator—sure, I'll start working out."

This can indeed be a real concern and barrier, but often it comes with an overestimation of how much time is necessary to really begin to change behavior. It's not difficult to carve out

15 minutes every day, but easier said than done.

Big fish, small pond. *"I'm good here. Don't worry about it."* toxic

If you're already doing well in your current environment, if you're operating at a level above other people in your immediate view—isn't that "good enough"? You're so much better than your everyone else in your surroundings that you don't understand why you need to improve. You're happy in your echo chamber, where nobody disagrees or offers your criticism, so as far as you're concerned, you're doing fine. "Why do I have to address my gambling problem? I beat every other guy in this town at Texas hold 'em!"

Plainly put, you are too comfortable or too insulated from negative consequences. This is not a bad thing, but it certainly doesn't make you hungry for change.

Harmful or opposing environment. *"He doesn't stop talking to me, so I can never get into a groove."*

Sometimes circumstances or settings have a damaging or highly uncomfortable effect on our natures or don't have what we require to start a program of change. A very introverted person might not be able to operate well in a crowded or loud place, or a person living in a very conservative community might feel discouraged about studying outside cultures. There are many ways our direct environments can impact us, and you'll read about them later.

Social inertia or rejection. *"No one else is doing it... and they might laugh at me and think I'm stupid!"*

This is an external manifestation of the confrontational avoidance and fear of rejection that we discuss above—however, we should also allow for the possibility that you're *not* merely paranoid. You very well may dwell in a social scene where people you see every day are profoundly disinterested in who you are or what you try to do and, in fact, are pretty much slackers themselves who are resistant to change on a group level. They have no interest themselves in change and actively drag you down to that level, belittling any effort or caring. That's social inertia.

Fears of rejection, on the other hand, might stem from fears that your change will disrupt the social order around you to the point where you're treated as an outcast. "If I start an exercise program, everybody I hang out with at the sports bar is going to tease me or think I'm working too hard." (Although if that's how they really think, you may just need to find better friends.)

So anyone who's thinking about starting a change in their lives is not at a loss for opposing forces, within or outside themselves. All of these forces—even the ones we don't notice or comprehend—can be conquered. It may look like a very tall order at the outset of your change program, but it's absolutely achievable. Understanding them is an important part of the battle. A doctor wouldn't operate without a clear understanding of what to remove, and attempting to forge ahead with behavior change without first introspecting is similarly foolhardy.

Getting started is usually the most foreboding part of the change process, and it depends on the strength and clarity of our motivation. That's what we'll address next.

Takeaways:

- Even though we logically and intellectually know what we should do, why don't do we those things? Because despite what we like to think, we aren't really operating on conscious free will most of the time. There are three categories of obstacles to really doing what we want at any point: *conscious, subconscious,* and *external* factors.

- Conscious factors are ones we know and readily tell ourselves. They are what we repeat when we fail or decide not to do something. They include low self-esteem, negative self-image, over-tolerance with pain or discomfort, aversion to confrontation, and fear of failure and rejection.

- Subconscious factors are similar to the conscious factors, yet they are so deeply ingrained in our identities we don't even realize we hold these beliefs—they are just our automatic thought patterns. They include limiting beliefs and narratives, having a fixed mindset, and being victim to traumatic experiences.

- External factors are outside of ourselves. They are the environmental or social pressures that keep us from taking action. Some of these are legitimate; some are simply excuses. These include lack of knowledge, too many obligations, too comfortable, harmful environments, social inertia, or rejection.

Chapter 3. What's Pushing You Forward?

What makes us want to do something, and how do we maintain that drive so we can finish what we start? As opposed to the previous chapter, what keeps us moving forward in the face of fear and pain?

Motivation is as mysterious and inexplicable a power as inspiration. It's hard to summon up and can be hard to sustain. And like the obstacles we discussed in the last chapter, motivation isn't directed by our logical abilities. If we were solely creatures of logic, motivation wouldn't even be necessary.

Rather, our motivation is as vulnerable to emotional change and stress as any other aspect of being human.

Motivation is important, but it also tends to wane after a fiery beginning. This is why, as you'll read later, rewriting your thought patterns, learning self-discipline, and creating new habits is the important part of making lasting changes. Motivation is certainly a part of behavior change, but only at the beginning, and not for sustained success. Relying on motivation is the same as relying on self-discipline and willpower—you can't force yourself to keep saying yes or no indefinitely. It also creates a very real learned helplessness, where you feel you can't act unless you are motivated, in the mood, or inspired. Motivation is a short-term solution—it's a helpful kickstart, but an emphasis on motivation is an emphasis on unsustainable practices.

Surprisingly, this is a shorter chapter than the chapter on mental obstacles for the simple reason that there is a much smaller realm of possible motivators for most people. Humans want very few things, or they can at least be reduced to a small number of dependable categories. Off the top of your head, you can probably name most types of motivations people will ever have. What keeps you moving is a slightly different story, as you'll read.

To address what can build proper motivation to change behavior, we can start with the exact same classifications we used in Chapter 2: conscious, subconscious, and external factors. The same things that hold us back can push us forward, and again, it's a matter of first identifying them.

Conscious Psychological Factors

Sometimes what motivates us can be fairly easy to understand on a conscious level. We want to feel positive emotions or create situations where we feel happiness.

We may use or even verbalize certain affirmations intended to spur us on: "I am successful," "The doors of opportunity are always open to me," "I enjoy challenges," or

"I deserve to be happy and I'm going to get it." What is more commonly known as a "pep talk" works because it lets you know directly what you are motivated by.

The most fundamental positive emotions we have—joy, achievement, satisfaction, pleasure, and general happiness—are all conscious motivators. We want to experience these, and we know when we feel them. They are pleasurable and we want them more and more.

But are they the most impactful for behavior change? Perhaps not. They are fairly shallow and surface-level, and chances are, seeking a positive reward isn't as motivating as avoiding heart-wrenching pain. Positive emotions can be motivations to *maintain* a behavior we want to keep, but to *change* something, we need to find a more active, deeper motivator.

Subconscious Psychological Factors

Again, many of our motivators exist outside of our awareness. They're hidden but powerful.

They're prompts to find ways to grow our happiness—or, perhaps more likely, reduce our unhappiness. Most of our subconscious motivators stem from negative or adverse feelings, in efforts to make ourselves feel better. There's nothing wrong with that on paper, but identifying them can be very useful.

Insecurity drivers. *"I just have to prove to others that I'm good enough."*

No subconscious stimulus may be more compelling than preserving our ego and combating our inadequacies. The harried office worker clocking overtime to prove themselves to a domineering boss. That boss purchasing a foreign sports car to ease doubts about his manhood. The salesman who aggressively sold him that car, trying to overcome his father's cutting remarks that he'd never be successful.

Insecurities nick away at our sense of pride and ego. If they don't derail us altogether, then they spur us to do things that will make us feel competent or mend our dignity. We want to avoid the pain of feeling inadequate, no matter how much of a falsehood it is, so we push. The risk is that we'll overcompensate to mask our perceived failings—which can be treacherous—the person who was called slow crashing into a tree while going 50 miles over the speed limit.

When you have "a chip on your shoulder," you seek approval from others and want to prove that you are as good or better than others. Despite whatever the reality is, you always feel like others are looking down on you —thus, you push hard to take action and change people's minds. They're all ways that we try to mask or kill the pain of not being enough. Many an eating disorder has been caused by subconscious insecurities from being told you were overweight as a child.

Confirming self-identity, avoiding cognitive dissonance. *"I am that trait, and I'll do this to prove it!"*

On the other hand, we may be driven to build up the positive parts of our identities. We work extra hard to confirm how we like to view ourselves. For instance, if we believe ourselves to be kind and giving, we will be fairly motivated to continue to confirm those self-perceptions and engage in kind and giving acts. Very few people believe they are bad people, and most believe they are good. We will work hard to keep our self-identity positive and true. This is both social pressure as well as internal pressure.

But in this area, there's always the risk of cognitive dissonance. Cognitive dissonance is when we have conflicting beliefs in our minds, and alleviating cognitive dissonance is when we reconcile the two conflicting beliefs with a circuitous story. For instance, if you said you hated all sports except soccer, you would reconcile these beliefs with a story about how soccer is special by nature.

Thus, if we view ourselves a certain way, kind and generous, and act in a way that appears to be opposite, we can too easily create a story to make both realities possible. Or if we run into hard evidence that disproves our most cherished beliefs, we scramble to find ways to relieve the friction that emerges. For instance, if we are kind and generous but have never donated to charity and never give friends gifts, you might reconcile these two conflicting beliefs with a story about how you have a special, unique kind of generosity and kindness. As you can imagine, this is the opposite of motivating.

External and Environmental Motivators

When we talk about external motivators, we're talking about influencing our surroundings to make us happier or less unhappy. As with everything, this operates on the pain-pleasure principle, which is far stronger from external sources. We want our physical and social environments to cater to our needs and whims.

These are perhaps the most reliable and consistent motivators we use on a daily basis. In fact, if you have a job, you are using them.

If you like eating, you are using them. If you like traveling and eating, you are using them. These are universal motivators, but not often the most important ones to people. In fact, people appear to be less driven by so-called shallow and material rewards after a certain threshold.

Material wealth, possessions, status and power. *"I'll do it if I get something big in return."*

Money and influence are classic incentives for amending personal behavior. We want them, they make us feel good about ourselves, and they allow us to literally change and rearrange our realities. But there's another benefit to having money and big house—the social validation we get from others.

We work for a paycheck so we can pay our rent and buy dinner. We seek promotions because we want better food and a bigger home. Eventually, material possessions are not enough, and we want power and influence over other people as well.

Not all of us have such lofty goals, but it is foolhardy to ignore how powerful of a motivator this can be. We work for a paycheck, but for instance, what kind of debauchery would you be willing to engage in for one million dollars? What kind of purchases or indulgences flashed through your mind? That question alone tells you how powerfully motivating external means are.

If this is you, there's nothing wrong with that. In fact, you'd be better served to embrace it fully so you can focus on what honestly drives you forward. For every Mother Teresa, we need a Steve Jobs as well, and happiness is subjective. If you find that something that makes you happy might be looked down upon by the rest of society, and that is keeping you from doing it, you might be more motivated by the next point.

Social validation, approval, acceptance, and love. *"If I do this, people will love me more."*

We care what people think. Some of us let this make all of our decisions for us. And it's not just our friends and family we care about. We care about anyone who will see us and anyone who has the potential for seeing us. This is a result of the spotlight effect, where we feel that everyone is always watching and judging us.

Thus, we act in ways that we think people will enjoy or approve of us, and sometimes this is actually detrimental to us. Yet still, it can be a strong motivator to avoid shame and win influence. This of course is the root of social anxiety and all forms of feeling awkward around others. You might know someone who cares so deeply what people think that they are perpetually frozen so they don't attract negative attention.

Seeking social validation and acceptance has been ingrained in us because humans are social creatures who have lived in tribes and empires for many generations. Risking shame was tantamount to a death sentence and banishment from the tribe. It's not a life or death situation anymore, but a lack of social validation does make us feel terrible.

Maslow's Hierarchy of Needs

Aside from the three categories of motivations, a universal set of motivations stems from what's known as Maslow's hierarchy of needs. Each stage of the hierarchy represents a unique set of motivations that can differ from person to person depending on the stage they are in.

The hierarchy was proposed by Abraham Maslow in the 1940s and was a theory based on the idea that human beings are a product of a set of basic human needs (and motivations), the deprivation of which is the primary cause of most psychological problems. The hierarchy is more similar to a ladder—if you aren't able to satisfy the first stages, you'll be preoccupied by them and won't be able to be bothered with the next stages.

The first stage is **physiological fulfillment**. This is when you're motivated by having a roof over your head and food on your table. Without security in these aspects, it is difficult for anyone to be motivated toward anything else. It would actually be harmful to them to be motivated by other things. This is logical because nothing else matters to you if you are homeless or starving.

The second stage is **safety**. Once someone has physiological fulfillment, they are motivated to ensure that it persists. They are motivated by the need for safety, security, and a lack of constant fear and anxiety. This is the feeling that imminent harm is not just around the corner. Unfortunately, many people never make it out of these first two stages due to unfortunate circumstances, so you can see why some people plainly aren't interested or motivated by other things.

The third stage is **love and belonging**. Now that your survival is ensured, you'll find that it is relatively empty without sharing it with people that you care about. Humans are social creatures, and you'll be motivated to effectuate that. This includes relationships with your friends and family and socializing enough so you don't feel that you are failing in your social life. This is where you want to feel like part of a community and have a social support system.

The fourth stage is **self-esteem**. At this stage, you are less motivated by simply *having* relationships. You want them to be good, mutually beneficial relationships that allow you to both feel good about yourself, as well as feel respected and beloved by others. You can look at this stage as the motivation for social validation and admiration.

The final stage is **self-actualization**. Once you reach this level, you start living outside of yourself. You start being motivated by impact and significance, in part because you don't need to account for yourself anymore. This is when you are able to live for something higher than yourself and your needs.

You want to become the best version of yourself, whatever that looks like to you. You want to grow and have simply the best experiences you can. You are motivated to connect with principles that require you to step beyond what is convenient and what is comfortable. This is the plane of morality, creativity, spontaneity, lack of prejudice, and acceptance of reality.

Self-actualization is placed at the top of the pyramid because this is the highest (and last) motivation people have. All the lower levels have to be met first before a person can reach this last level. This is the stage people are at when they say they want to find their calling and purpose in life.

As you can see, there are multiple types of motivations that can push us toward our goals of changing our behavior. Just remember that they might not get you where you want to go.

Takeaways:

- Though motivations are important, motivations won't get you to your goals—they are short-term solutions to long-term problems. An emphasis on motivation is an emphasis on unsustainable practices.
- The same three categories apply with motivations as with obstacles: conscious, subconscious, and external.
- Conscious motivations include our positive emotions and positioning ourselves to experience them, while subconscious motivations include compensating for insecurity and confirming your self-identity. External motivations are the ways we experience the world around us, from social relationships, to money, to power, to our surroundings.
- Finally, Maslow's hierarchy of needs represents a set of universal motivations that accurately portray why people are preoccupied or *stuck*. The stages of the hierarchy are physiological fulfillment, safety, love and belonging, self-esteem, and self-actualization. Many people will never make it through the entire hierarchy.

Chapter 4. Start Your Engines

The planning's over, your inventory's finished, and it's time to start the actual work toward changing your behavior. This is precisely the point where many of us rev up our engines and then... hurry up and wait.

For many of us, the hardest part of launching a project is breaking out of inaction and getting to work. It doesn't matter that we've got everything we need in front of us or that we've been waiting days for no apparent reason for blastoff. This is incidentally when our bathrooms will be cleaned and our carpets will be vacuumed. *At least if we're avoiding something, we can do something vaguely productive in the meantime.*

Simply starting is the *biggest* step you'll be making this whole process: switching from "off" to "on." In a sense, it is difficult because you are switching from virtually nothing to something—a mathematical increase of infinite. It's easier to go from one to one hundred, even, because that's only a mathematical increase of 100x, and you have the benefit of building up momentum. Starting is jumping out of the nest, jumping into the deep end, igniting a flame, and any number of other analogies.

Not only is it difficult from a practical and momentum perspective, but it's also difficult from a fear perspective. We don't really know what we're going to face, even if we've planned meticulously for months. It is inherently out of your comfort zone and sphere of experience. Things might go wrong (what in the world will you do then?), and all of your plans might need to go out the window. And, of course, you are leaving the security of a cocoon and opening yourself up to failure and rejection. This is the tipping point where you have to close your eyes and hold your breath for a bit while you take a small leap of faith.

The associated uncertainty can be terrifying, but it is literally impossible to feel the certainty you want for something you've never experienced before. It comes with the territory.

You might even have the best of intentions but are unintentionally procrastinating.

Procrastination

Procrastination will definitely keep you from starting, but perhaps not in the way you might expect. Perfectionism is a type of procrastination. Procrastination has a simple definition: delaying commencement of a project until the last possible moment. Perfectionism is the natural extension and also holds up our actions and keeps us stagnant.

Perfectionism is sometimes called "the highest form of self-abuse." Striving for perfection is unreasonable almost by definition because it doesn't even exist. The concern that we must carry out all of our activities as seamlessly and blemish-free as we can—or we don't do it at all—keeps us from getting started. It keeps us from taking a chance with half-formed ideas or working without a net and forces us to stay where it's safe and convenient and where nobody offers any criticism.

Procrastination is a *symptom* of perfectionism. Since perfectionists fear not completing their tasks perfectly, they simply put it off for as long as they can. They feel that not meeting their prescribed goals means there's something bad, wrong, or unworthy about them. They fear that failure will involve criticism or ridicule from either internal or external voices. The acuter that fear gets, the longer perfectionists procrastinate.

One thing that should be made clear is that procrastination and laziness aren't the same thing. Indeed, if there's anything giving procrastinators any fuel, paradoxically, it's their burning desire to work *well*. They have a low tolerance for frustration and failure—but for them, procrastination has become the activity through which they channel those anxieties. When they feel the standards are sky-high and perceive accomplishment to be outside their capabilities, they sidestep the discomfort through diversion.

Besides, you already know that perfection is almost never achievable in any endeavor. You know that nobody's perfect, no project is perfect, and nothing ever goes 100% perfectly in any situation. So calling yourself a "perfectionist" is just an excuse: you think it's not possible, so you don't even start. You're not a perfectionist with exacting standards; you're just insulating yourself from discomfort and change.

Perfectionism is also wrapped up in what we *believe* other people's expectations of us are. This desire for external approval can lead us toward inactivity because if we're not doing anything, then nobody can see us fail. But you have to remember the most likely truth:

nobody's watching, nobody cares, and nobody else matters, primarily because they're so wrapped up with themselves that they won't notice mistakes you might make. Let your desire to impress others go and try to decouple your performance from your sense of self-worth.

Furthermore, realize there's a crucial difference between perfection and excellence. Striving for excellence is a normal, healthy drive based on performing at your best. In stark contrast, perfectionism is a negative emotion working from a fear of mistakes or insufficiency. Excellence is independent of that.

Remember that perfectionism is an unrealistic, unobtainable thing—it can only keep you from acting upon something and give you excuses not to act.

Another covert form of procrastination is endless rumination—analyzing, assessing, inventing, predicting, and otherwise appraising potential actions rather than actually getting up and *doing* the thing.

Many companies, including some of the most successful in the world, sometimes find themselves wrangling over "meeting culture." This is where multiple, fact-finding conferences are scheduled, often one right after the other. There are jump-off meetings, weekly staff meetings, department meetings, and personal one-on-one meetings. Sometimes scheduled meetings are nothing more than checkpoints to find out how a certain project is progressing. Well, the project *would* be progressing quite nicely if you didn't have to attend all these meetings.

You have to have occasional meetings, of course. But in the end, they're simply an abstraction of work, not the actual execution of work—meaning, simply, there's a lot of planning going on at these conferences and nobody actually picking up the actual shovel, so to speak.

This notion is parallel to what we call "planning paralysis"—when planning becomes a higher priority than actually *doing* something. The job of *planning* to takes precedence over, or at least valuable time from, your actual project.

Ultimately, it's another form of procrastination. Gathering more information than you absolutely need, conducting multiple analyses of different ways to achieve something, combing over minute and usually unnecessary details, debating back and forth in your own head about multiple scenarios—all of these actions are used as something that will postpone your taking action. After all, it's easier to plan than do.

For example, you can spend hours in a recliner leafing through cooking websites to find better ways of making a particular dish. You might find a perfectly decent recipe but then see another one that might be more interesting. You can keep on looking up additional recipes and maybe even stumble upon a side dish you'd like to make as well. You find a lot of possibilities, and they all look fairly good. Next thing you know, it's five minutes before dinnertime and you haven't so much as filled a pot with water. And on top of it all, the very first recipe you looked at may have been more than sufficient.

Planning precisely isn't the worst way to go about projects. But more likely, planning is a device that helps one avoid action to mollify our fears and anxieties. You will never feel truly ready when you engage in something new, and over-planning is simply avoidance.

An easy heuristic to combat procrastination, perfectionism, and over-planning is dubbed the 75% rule. Simply, take action when you're only about 75% certain you'll be correct or successful. The truth is, you'll never be 100% certain, and typically when you're at 75% you are more than ready and even begin to have diminishing returns. Just round up and you're there. Remember, you will never feel the ultimate certainty you wish for with a new endeavor.

If you feel there is a 75% chance you can complete a task, that is more than enough for you to act on. Note that it is a 75% chance of completing the task, not completing the task "successfully" or "perfectly." If at the beginning you are measuring your progress by how well you perform, versus simply performing, your expectations are a bit skewed.

Are you procrastinating subconsciously?

SMART Goals

Another method to get off your butt and finally put pen to paper is to formulate effective goals. Goals seem easy to set, but in reality, there are many ways of articulating your goals that will keep you frozen in motion.

Businessman Paul J. Meyer, who founded Success Motivation International, outlined the concept of "SMART goals," an acronymic checklist that helps to assess whether the goals one establishes are achievable. Suffice it to say, using his framework will push you into action sooner rather than later. He arranged the criteria into five areas of examination:

Specific. The goals you set should be precise and unambiguous, or you won't have a clear definition of what you need to accomplish and won't be strongly driven to achieve your aims. Meyer breaks down this analysis to six simple questions based on six interrogative "W's" used by journalists:

- *Why* is the goal important to you?

- *Who* needs to be involved to achieve this goal?

- *What* exactly do you need to accomplish?

- *Which* requirements, obstacles, or methods are necessary to deal with to get you to your goal?

- *Where* do you need to go to get your goals going? (This may not always be necessary to ask.)

These answers don't have to go too far "in the weeds," but they should be clear enough to serve as a statement of purpose and mission. Let's use a common and popular behavioral change as an example of the SMART goals track: establishing a workout routine. The answers to some of these questions should be fairly obvious:

- Why? Because you want to live healthier.

- Who's involved? You, for one. Maybe a personal trainer, too.

- What do you need to accomplish? Building strength and/or losing or gaining weight.

- Which requirements or obstacles do you deal with? You need to establish a routine and use gymnasium equipment. Your obstacles could be personal—self-consciousness in a workout environment or living a bit far from a useful gym facility.

- Where do you need to go to do this? If the gym's too far, maybe there's a space in your house you can clear for working out—or you could just focus on activities you can do anywhere, like running or biking.

Measurable. Keeping track of your advancement through your goal is a huge part of remaining motivated. Recording your progress step by step will keep you fully aware of how much you've accomplished and how far you have to go, especially when you're in the latter stages and trying to keep momentum.

Workouts, in particular, thrive on keeping records of your progress: how many reps you do, how many miles you run or bike, by how much you increase your effort over a period of time, how much weight or size you're losing or gaining on a weekly basis, and how far away you are from your targets. If you don't measure it, you won't know it, and you won't do it.

Achievable. Be pragmatic about setting your expectations. Although it's important to stretch your capabilities to grow, your goal should be something you can actually complete. You probably won't rise into a senior executive position if you've only been with a company for six weeks or even six months. Careful estimation of what's realistically possible for you in a modest time frame will help you build your resources gradually and chart your success more surely. If your goal is too easy, you will be bored and unmotivated. If your goal is too difficult, you will become discouraged and quit.

For the workout regimen, results should be achievable according to several factors. Your body build may not support dramatic weight loss or gain, so know what you can expect to achieve, perhaps working from the perspective of getting healthier and changing dietary habits. You're probably going to need to set a workout regimen that fits into your daily schedule and moderate your expectations according to what you can accomplish in that timetable.

Relevant. Do you feel like your goal actually matters? Is it a useful or worthwhile pursuit? Does it fill an established need? Is now the best time to be following this track, or might it be too soon? Is it something that will be valuable in the current personal climate? And are you the best person to bring it to reality?

For the workout example, this isn't a terribly difficult dilemma. Getting healthy is obviously a worthy quest and fills a need. You're of course the best person to make it happen. You could conceivably have a few time-related fixes to think about—there might be a practical reason for you to wait a couple of weeks. Or none at all.

Time-bound. This is a deadline. This could be an additional "when" question in the "specific" category but deserves its own mention. (Plus, we need a "T" section to finish the acronym anyway.) You need to set a due date or deadline to measure your milestones and keep your focus on the finish line. Of course, this is critical to avoiding procrastination. Set your expectations along a certain time frame. When should you finish the job? What can you do right now, in six months, and in six weeks?

In terms of our workout routine, what size or weight can you expect to be after a certain amount of time (two weeks, six months, a year)? Base your expectations on the other factors in your SMART goal assessment—but once you make a deadline or numeric goal, stick to it.

Turn Boulders into Pebbles

Part of the dread we might feel at the onset of any project or change might be its sheer magnitude.

A problem that looks too taxing or large could make you feel doomed from the start. That doesn't mean it isn't manageable, though—it just means you need to break it down into smaller components that are easier to execute. By breaking down the job into smaller chunks, you make it simpler to control and easier to keep the drive alive.

The best way to get rolling on a big project is to divide it into smaller parts as quickly as possible. I admit up front that it's not easy. We've been assigned tasks that seemed like colossal time drains that snag up a lot of our energies. Just thinking about how enormous it is can be fatiguing, and our first impulse might be to avoid it and scan our Facebook and Twitter timelines to see if there have been any updates in the last five minutes.

The longer we put off what needs our attention, the more the tension builds and the more complicated the project becomes. It is a monster that keeps amplifying in size, and it becomes even more formidable than it looked in the beginning. That's why it's better to start breaking up the project into smaller pieces before too much time has gone by.

When you're first looking at this gigantic thing, just stand back and make a rough analysis of how many parts it can be broken down into. What are they, and what will they really require to get done? Make sure you write down the individual components, think them through, and start with the ones that are easiest to get done. Getting a couple of quick and easy wins notched on your belt from the start can be a great source of early momentum for the harder things to come.

Break down your task into incremental goals: daily, weekly, and monthly. How would this task incorporate into your daily routine? What are some of the less work-heavy parts you can do that would have greater effects on the big picture? And what steps can you omit?

Major accomplishments don't just happen with the wave of a magic wand and the sudden appearance of a giant problem-solving machine in the middle of your home or office. All of them are made up of the results of a bunch of smaller jobs performed at a reasonable speed with relative ease.

To get something going in this way, ask yourself the following questions. As an example of how they'll work, let's say you're learning how to code with the intent of building out a full website for your own business. These questions make very clear how you can get started on something seemingly huge.

What would you Google first to get this problem solved? The beauty of modern search technology is how immediately you can get a layman's knowledge about virtually any topic. Thinking in the model of a search engine keeps your perspective on a smaller scale. From there, you can build a fuller outline much more easily.

For our example—well, if a web search engine can't help you find quick info on how to get started building a website, it's the worst search engine in the history of tech and you shouldn't invest time or money in it. If you Google the programming language "HTML," the first result that pops up is a free HTML tutorial at W3Schools. "Website building" brings up lots of hosting companies, but that may be for further down the road. Still good to know. "How to code" brings up information that's more useful for your creative goals, like intensive online learning sites and articles about how to teach yourself code.

These three very simple, very brief strings have given you a free tutorial, a possible virtual classroom or framework, and some place that might host your site when you're ready. Not bad for five minutes of light typing.

If you only had 10 minutes to make progress on this every day this week, what would you do? You can't put too many burdens on yourself about how massive or time-consuming your project will be in total—that's a great way to keep you from doing anything now. So to counteract this, start considering the job in very, *very* small terms. You won't have to get everything done in one shot. Think about how much you can complete on the project in small portions at a time—they *will* add up.

For our coding example, you'd probably get a lot out of those daily 10 minutes. You could teach yourself a new command each day. You could investigate color combinations that will work. You could do a quick comparison of pricing for competing web servers. Or you could practice a writing sample. (I'm pretty certain the creative and financial structure of the blog support articles were written in 10 minutes, probably less.)

What are the unknowns? What do I need to do to know them? If you can identify the gaps in knowledge or functionality that are keeping a project in neutral, you can make clear what you need to research and who you need to engage to fill them up. It can also help you reinforce what you *already* know and what you have the skills and abilities to work on now. Like the other functions in your overarching task, research and study are projects that can be broken down into smaller or shorter jobs.

Meanwhile, back at your website, you might be inclined to note some of the ornate styles or functions of bigger businesses' online presences and felt intimidated by the idea of putting them together. There's one area you could learn about. You don't know the different programming languages that are all supposed to work together in a complex website. You might be shaky on making your site mobile-friendly first. And you might not know exactly what you need to do to turn your blog into a revenue generator. Write these chasms down and go looking.

What's my definition of "small and manageable"? There may be parts of the big task you already have considerable expertise and experience with. But for someone not in your shoes, these tasks may be larger and heavier. Make sure you're measuring the size and difficulty against your range of abilities as they currently are.

Remember, they'll be different for everyone. Try not to be too self-critical about your abilities in comparison to someone else who has a little more experience—what you can manage now is just fine. You'll get better and more skillful as you learn.

Let's finish off our website example. Are you a hunt-and-peck typist or can you dash off 100 words a minute? That might affect how much code you can crank out in a given period of time and how much you'll have to rely on tools to generate code. Do you have a physical business to manage, in addition to all your other personal responsibilities? That might impact your time as well. Or you could be a blazing typist with nothing much going on in your professional or personal life—so you might be able to race your way to cyber glory in no time.

Embrace the Beginner's Mindset

No matter what amount of experience you might have in a particular skill, there's value in approaching a new project from the standpoint of someone who, relatively speaking, has no idea what they're doing. Incidentally, this is helpful in starting your engines because of the embracing of failure beginners have.

How does one best approach projects as an absolute beginner? By moderating their expectations, not anticipating immediate fortune without putting in the required work, and not counting on instant change. Beginners have a lot of time in front of them to work on a project, which is good—because time is what that endeavor will require. They understand that there is a process and that there will be failure along the path.

Having moderate (most usually *lower*) expectations can be a key to happiness. Zen monk Shunryu Suzuki once explained, "In the beginner's mind there are many possibilities, but in the expert's mind there are few." The reasoning is easy to see: when we're young we have no experience, so we believe that anything is possible. That leads to more experimentation, more wonder, more openness, and less determinism. And *real* experts know that all those qualities are important to bring to a project—even if they already know more than most others about that project.

Beginners aren't married to certain ways of thinking; they're willing to embrace the untried, uncomfortable, or just plain strange. They're willing to be led in that direction because they still know that they *don't* know. They're open and don't have bad habits they defend out of stubbornness. They expect to fumble their way around and face failure and frustration on a daily basis. This is the reality of new endeavors, and even Mozart or Beethoven had to learn how to read music at first.

Getting started in itself is not a difficult task, but as with everything involving behavior change, there are always a plethora of psychological reasons we do not move forward. To get started, you either have to want something badly enough or be miserable enough. Whichever is your motivation, this chapter will help kickstart you into action.

Takeaways:

- Getting started on changing your behavior is the most difficult part because it involves confronting fear, uncertainty, and making a leap of faith.

- Aside from the psychological reasons, you may also be unwittingly procrastinating. Perfectionism and over-planning are forms of covert procrastination because they allow us to keep spinning our wheels from the comfort of never starting. Beware that you are not using these as excuses to yourself.

- SMART goals are helpful in getting started because it is too easy to set goals that actually detract from your motivation. SMART goals consist of five aspects: specific, measurable, attainable, relevant, and time-bound.

- Seek to break your tasks into as small of tasks as possible in order to reduce intimidation and simply make it easy to do something—anything. Break boulders into pebbles and see that every boulder is simply composed of nearly weightless pebbles that you can move at a moment's notice. You can ask yourself any of the questions ("What can I Google right now?") to see the types of small tasks you can immediately engage in.

- Embrace the beginner's mindset, because it will help temper your expectations and keep you open-minded to the possibility of failure. Beginners often fail—why wouldn't they? It would be odd if they didn't. Therefore, if you don't expect to succeed linearly, getting started suddenly seems much easier.

Chapter 5. Maintain Momentum

We associate momentum with the notion of an accelerating force: a rolling motivator fueled by desire and incremental victories that keep us going toward the finish line. It's an intangible push that breezes us over obstacles and keeps us from regressing. Momentum is an even stronger stimulus the further you are from the start of your project, because it gains as you practice and advance your skills.

The best part is that momentum is self-perpetuating. When we feel it, we *feel* it; we are in the *zone*.

But momentum's more delicate than one might imagine. It walks a fine line and requires a certain type of maintenance, lest it be knocked off course completely. You can't push too hard, and you can't lose yourself too completely for the same reason you can't push too much electrical current through a power line.

In the context of behavior change, momentum is how you keep going after an initial spark of motivation. It's how you push through what's to come, bad times, discouraging times, and the pain of failure. It's how you will yourself to get back up after getting knocked down. It's how you see your goals through to the end and actually change the behavior you want.

But it's not enough to know that you should seek momentum. You need to keep a presence of mind for certain pitfalls associated with momentum.

Avoid burnout. At least during the initial phase of a project, you can't just toil away for 24 hours a day without interruption.

You need to take a break the way athletes need time to recover and rest from exercise and competition. More than just a reprieve, this time off needs to restore your mental and physical states. Without it, you run the risk of burning out and possibly stopping for good due to your connecting the work with bad feelings.

Driving yourself to avoid inactivity and make progress is one thing; over-extending yourself to the point of collapse is quite another. Have you ever tried to read a book but ended up having to read the same paragraph five times because you can't focus on it? There's simply a point of diminishing returns where anything you continue to do in your tired state will have to be redone or reread anyway.

This is one area in which keeping a record of your progress can be of great help. Besides having an account of how far you've come, it also gives you the chance to ease off a bit by reminding you how much you've accomplished so far. Instead of just laboring under the general idea that you have to keep pushing yourself because you haven't done anything, by keeping track, you have solid proof of what you've completed. No progress is too insignificant—so include the small things as well as the major milestones. <u>You may not feel compelled to keep pushing if you understand the number of hours you already put in.</u>

Seeing evidence of your progress is easy with certain visual art or manufacturing projects, but it's not always so with behavioral changes or long-term projects. In those cases, keeping a journal is a nearly failsafe tool. If you're working on getting healthy, chart your progress every day: calories saved, exercise reps counted, measurable health factors like weight and blood pressure recorded. If you're shifting to a new career, make quick notes at the end of the day that describe your activities, explain new concepts you've just learned, and identify questions or new challenges you need to find answers for.

Avoid pointlessness. Tasks that don't have clear objectives, purposes, or reasons can hold back all the aspects of any project, including momentum. If you can't identify the payoff of your work, the end that you're working toward, then what's the point? "Busy work" doesn't have any place in major activity; more often than not it's just to give the appearance of effort but doesn't contribute anything real. Every step in a major effort needs to be justified with real targets and results. At any point during your behavior changes, you should be able to answer the simple question of "Why am I doing this?"

One example of a pointless activity in the business is excessive deliberation, more charmingly referred to as "analysis paralysis." Sure, having strategy sessions and taking the temperature of a project is important—but getting stuck in that mode can be a killer de-motivator. At some point, you have to accept what you can't micromanage and give a green light, rather than spend unproductive hours at a constantly flashing yellow one.

In changing behavior, there's a trap in having too many stray activities that at first seem organized toward the goal but might not make much of a final contribution in the long run. Some of your exercise routines might not be doing anything to your muscles or cardiovascular system other than making you aware that you have them—learn which ones really have the most impact and leave the rest out. Is what you're engaging in really impacting, or is it being done for an arbitrary reason?

Avoid boredom. When we are trying to accomplish something, we get bored in two main instances: if it is too easy or it is too hard. If it is too easy, it's not challenging, and our attention flows to something that will keep you engaged. If it is too difficult, you become too discouraged and give up. The way to avoid boredom is to find the optimal level of stress that encourages engagement and top performance. This level is achieved when you are alert and engaged, but not overly fearful, and just a slight step outside of your comfort zone.

Finding the sweet spot is predicated on how physiologically aroused you are in the moment. If you are too aroused, you become stressed out, and you are bound to overthink the situation and mess up. If you aren't aroused enough (bored or uninterested), you aren't alert enough to pay attention because you simply don't care. The balance between these extremes is the sweet spot where you function at your best and are most engaged.

The most famous method for measuring the optimal level of stress, the so-called sweet spot, was defined in 1908 by Robert Yerkes and John Dodson. They designed a graph in the shape of an upside-down U that demonstrates how our performance on a task will be poor when we are disengaged (uninterested), but as our arousal rises, our performance improves until it reaches the sweet spot—the Yerkes-Dodson Curve. Beyond that point, further arousal becomes a handicap. The stress becomes debilitating, and our performance suffers.

Image courtesy of ResearchGate

Imagine a golfer who has just hit a hole in one. That is an extremely difficult feat and not likely to be repeated during a single round. But he puts the pressure on himself to perform, feeling rigid and tense with the effort. Suddenly, he's incapable of making a three-foot putt, much less scoring another hole in one. He is too aroused, the alertness turns to great stress, and he chokes.

The goal in regards to focus is to find your optimal level of challenge where you don't feel bored but don't feel like you are tackling something impossible. This is what will keep you engaged, moving forward, and focused. You can do this in two ways.

First, you can manipulate how challenging tasks are to you. Of course, we don't always have the option of choosing what to work on, but you can change how challenging or easy a task is by giving yourself shorter or longer deadlines or ways to compete against yourself to give an otherwise easy task purpose and vigor. For instance, challenging yourself to write more or lose more weight in less time will create more *good* stress.

Second, you can design your work to alternate between easy and difficult tasks to keep you engaged and never too over- or underwhelmed. As mentioned, it's not often we can control that which we are trying to focus on, so at least we can spread out our stress strategically and avoid boredom.

Pace Yourself

Momentum is frequently correlated with speed, like a stone rolling down a hill, getting faster as it nears the bottom. But that's not the whole ball of wax—if the uncontrolled stone runs into a tree on its way down, so much for its momentum.

Lasting changes are not just a matter of quickness; it's also about moderating the pace so the job gets done right. That's why pacing yourself is crucial. Here are some thoughts on managing the rate and tempo of your work.

Parkinson's law. "Work expands to fill the time available for its completion." Those of you familiar with productivity recognize that adage as Parkinson's law. It was formed by Cyril Parkinson, a British historian, who first used it as the opening statement in an article he wrote for *The Economist*. It also served as the nucleus of his book *Parkinson's Law: The Pursuit of Progress.*

It's explained like this: if you allow yourself a week to complete a job that would normally take two hours, the task will get more intricate and involved in a psychological sense. Even though you've given yourself more time to complete the job, it won't give you the "break" you might think you'll get.

Instead, it will get more intimidating as the week progresses. That week will get filled up *somehow*—if not with more work, then with the pressure to get the job done.

Just give yourself exactly as much time you will need to accomplish your assignment, and avoid making the "buffer" time too long. That will streamline your schedule and give you time back. The complexity of the task—and the anxiety associated with getting it done—will contract back to its true, natural state.

On the other hand, don't try and get everything out the door at once. Rushing through a series of jobs can affect the quality and effectiveness of your work, possibly causing gaps or shortfalls that you might have to come back to fix later. *That* will negate the momentum you thought you were accelerating by doing too much too soon. Give yourself a reasonable period of time for every step you execute—short enough to ensure efficiency but long enough to get it as right as you can.

Taking breaks. We've already mentioned the importance of having breaks. But there's a certain way to take breaks called "combinatory play." It's so good that it was even approved by Albert Einstein.

The most notable scientist of the 20th century was known for taking time out of his work to play the violin. Reportedly, he was even very good at it, as he was with the piano. But while sawing away on the violin during his breaks, Einstein actually arrived at some breakthroughs in his research and philosophical questionings. Allegedly one of these musical sessions was the spark for his most famous equation: $E=mc^2$.

Einstein came up with the term "combinatory play" to describe the intangible process in which his favorite pastime led to ideas that revolutionized the whole of scientific thought. He explained his reasoning as best he could in 1945, in a letter to French mathematician Jacques S. Hadamard:

> "The desire to arrive finally at logically connected concepts is the emotional

> basis of this rather vague play with the above-mentioned elements. But taken from a psychological viewpoint, this combinatory play seems to be the essential feature in productive thought—before there is any connection with logical construction in words or other kinds of signs which can be communicated to others... Conventional words or other signs have to be sought for laboriously only in a secondary stage when the mentioned associative play is sufficiently established and can be reproduced at will... The play with the mentioned elements is aimed to be analogous to certain logical connections one is searching for."

Einstein wasn't satisfied with his own explanation, which we can kind of understand: there's an element of mystery to the creative act of playing music, and trying to explain it can be seen as fruitless. But that makes his own point—that before a certain breakthrough can be logically said, it has to be discovered on an emotional or intuitive level. In other words, it has to happen and you have to feel it before you define it. When Einstein took breaks to play music, some of these concepts first presented themselves to him. He'd play through and would work out how to explain them later.

It's fine to take breaks and yield your brain to the occasional meaningless diversion. We all need breaks like that to reset ourselves. But you could also investigate how to incorporate combinatory play into your break time. We all need downtime—but it's fine if even the smallest bit of productivity can come from it.

Schedule in your behavior changes. Ever hear that consistency is the root of all change?

It's true. If you don't use it, you lose it. That's why scheduling your changes into your day at least gives you a fighting chance of keeping them up. Prioritize this time as holy and make others schedule around it, not you. That's the only way you know that you are actually prioritizing what you want over what others want.

Schedule this daily, and it must never be canceled or postponed except in the case of natural disaster or medical emergency—this is another test of your resolve. What obstacles will you allow to get in the way of your behavior change commitment? It doesn't have to be for an hour; in fact, scheduling in only small doses is much more palatable psychologically. Seeing an hour block on your calendar can be a little deflating, and you will start to associate it with a dragging chore. On the other hand, seeing a 15-minute block feels lightweight and almost effortless, which is ultimately good for pace-setting and keeping momentum. It's also easy to overshoot your smaller goals.

Plan to fail. Failure is conflated with disappointment and let-down—but in actuality, it's a routine part of progress and making changes. Nothing is ever a one-shot success out of the box. And not only should failure *not* be seen through the lens of devastation, but it should also be something *expected* and planned for. This is not being pessimistic about your endeavors: it's accounting for a negative result and learning where adjustments need to be made. Build this expectation into your timelines and you'll feel better about yourself when your progress isn't wholly linear—which is impossible.

For behavior change, it's not important to be perfect (and it's also impossible)—what matters is that you're *consistent*. Many weight-loss programs allow for "cheat days," that one day a week when you can go relatively crazy on eating. Writers, even the most famous or successful ones, have to get used to getting rejection letters—sometimes their week doesn't feel *complete* without at least one. It's important that you're moving forward at the end of it all, despite slight setbacks or planned *failures*.

By incorporating the reality of failure into strategy, we not only learn more about what we want to change, but we also remove the stigma or embarrassment of failure—or at the very least make it hurt less.

Occasionally go fast and break things.
There's always an exception. Sometimes, it

benefits us to simply run as fast as possible, break things in our path, and see where we end up when we open our eyes. It can be slightly reckless and exhausting, but sometimes momentum is just that—seizing it as it comes and riding it until you can do no more with it. This is when you work until 5:00 a.m. simply because you're having a flash of inspiration, despite the fact that you will be a zombie at work the next day. Sometimes, this is worth it, and you should never cut yourself short if you are in that mood.

This seems like a natural inclination, but best-selling author Seth Godin explained the fears momentum can create and how those fears activate what he called our "lizard brain"—the part of our minds that is "sabotaging our projects just before we show them to the world":

> "Many of us fear too much momentum. We look at a project launch or a job or another new commitment as something that might get out of control. It's one thing to be a folk singer playing to a hundred people a night in a

> coffeehouse, but what if the momentum builds and you become a star? A rock star? With an entourage and appearances and higher than high expectations for your next work? … Deep down, this potential for an overwhelming response alerts the 'lizard brain' and we hold back."

Trepidations about going too fast with the stream of momentum are okay—but they should never exceed your sense of awe and appreciation that you have the chance to move forward. You can deal with the concerns any time, but when momentum hits, seize upon it and ride it. Take advantage of the energy instead of letting it drain *you*. After all, to make an omelet, you need to break some eggs.

Momentum can be the only chance you'll have to reach certain levels, thoughts, movements, or achievements. Will you let it pass you by?

Takeaways:

- Momentum is what keeps us persisting toward our goals even in hard times. Yet, it is hard to find and easy to be knocked off of.

- Momentum is most likely when you can avoid burnout, feelings of pointlessness, and boredom by understanding the Yerkes-Dodson curve.

- Pacing is also important to sticking with your behavior changes, and it involves understanding Parkinson's law, taking *combinatory play* breaks, scheduling for failure, scheduling and prioritizing your practice, and occasionally riding yourself to the brink of exhaustion just because you're in the zone.

Chapter 6. Correcting Course

You've ridden your momentum and likely made a load of progress. That's the hope, anyway. Once you're in the zone, you have the opportunity to forget about the troubles of your daily life and simply ride the wave. Of course, this is great in terms of distance, but not necessarily in terms of accuracy.

Let's take a rocket launch—it might go far and cover a lot of ground, but mini-corrections will have to be made and accounted for the entire way. It might not be 100% on course, even if it's blazing fast. This is all to say that no matter how quickly you can start to see progress in changing your behaviors, you will inevitably need to take a step back to evaluate how everything is going and make adjustments.

You've gotten this far, based on momentum or just plain grinding work, and now you're in the position to analyze what's working and what isn't. It may sound annoying and tedious, but you can look at it this way: most people never enter this stage of change! Most people fizzle out and never gain enough steam to take more than one step.

The fact is, your goals will be much more attainable if you get into the habit of looking for feedback, evaluating yourself, and gaining (objective) self-awareness of your progress. Things always look different when planning versus having started, so it's time to take what you've learned thus far into account.

This chapter addresses resources and ways to examine your progress and whether and how you need to change direction. Paying attention to yourself is one of the main difficult things in the world, but we're going to attempt to learn how.

Biofeedback

The first way to evaluate your progress and recognize whether changes need to be made to your process is *biofeedback*. Specifically, if you are pushing too hard and placing too many expectations on yourself, you're acting, but in a counterproductive way.

The word biofeedback brings to mind images from old sci-fi movies of subjects with electrodes stuck to their heads, with wires leading to a constantly beeping computer. That's one way of doing it, but in a broader sense, it just refers to the signals your body is sending you about what you're doing. By listening to our bodies, we are able to accurately assess whether something feels good, doesn't do enough, or pushes you too hard. *If it feels good, keep doing it; if it feels bad, it's time to change it up.*

In a literal sense, biofeedback measures your body's physical and physiological reactions as they're happening, and it provides mechanisms to regulate them. It's true that there's some technology involved in biofeedback: machines that gauge your blood pressure, pulse, muscular tension, and even brainwaves. But you don't require that technology if you learn how to measure those factors yourself.

The Institute of Psychiatry at King's College London hails biofeedback therapy as a "non-invasive, effective psycho-physiological intervention for psychiatric disorders." In over 80% of the studies they conducted, they found some notable declines in symptoms as an outcome of biofeedback—simply listening to their bodies. As a result, they've been able to treat patients who have experienced a wide range of psychological maladies, such as depression, schizophrenia, anxiety, and eating disorders.

Why exactly does listening to our bodies work? First, the simple knowledge that you are evaluating yourself is enough to cause a change. When a subject comprehends that they're just engaging in biofeedback, their stress responses are already becalmed through the relaxation methods they're using: meditation, deep breaking, and visualizations.

Our internal fight-or-flight response is reduced merely by understand that we should be relaxing more. Knowing how your body is operating can also help you understand what adjustments you need to make, what relaxation strategies are working, and which aren't—a significant aspect of behavioral change all on its own.

The second reason to listen to our bodies is because sometimes, our bodies are far wiser than our brains. They know what is better for us more than we think, and we shouldn't always push the boundaries to where we can mentally.

But you don't have to visit a psychiatric lab and get hooked up to a polygraph to conduct your own informal but still informative biofeedback analysis. What can we learn from our bodies in correcting the course of our behavioral changes? There are several factors you can track on your own:

Heart rate. Turn your wrist so your palms are facing up, and gently place two fingers (but not your thumb) perpendicular to the artery you see. Count how many pulses or beats you feel in 30 seconds. Your pulse rate is twice the number of beats you count. What constitutes a "normal" heart rate differs according to conditions like age, but in general, between 60 and 100 beats per minute is considered normal. Is your heart rate too fast? Too slow? Irregular? Any of those three are warning signs for physiological stress that could be impeding your progress.

Sleep quality and energy. Studies vary, but adults need somewhere around seven hours of sleep a night. Children need more, and elderly people need less. How much are you sleeping, and is it enough? Moreover, are you able to stay asleep without tossing and turning? Are you able to fall asleep without monkeys running through your mind all night? Often, an exhausted mind creates good, healthy sleep. However, a stressed and anxious mind creates fitful, interrupted sleep. Where are you on the spectrum?

The same goes for general levels of fatigue and energy throughout your day. When you are in a state of perpetual *arousal*—in this case *negative* because it relates to anxiety and worry—you are going to be trading off between alert and tired from being so alert. Your nervous system does not like that kind of ping pong action, and the stress accumulates. So again, where are you on the spectrum of sleep quality, and how does that translate to your energy during the day? If you feel that you sleep a lot and still need cups of coffee to wake up, you're in trouble.

Muscle tension. Did you know there is such a thing as a tension headache? A tension headache is a headache that, well, isn't really a headache at all. It starts from carrying tension in your shoulders and neck and spreads to your temples until it cripples you for hours. And it's completely avoidable. But if this is something you're doing unconsciously, as well as feeling physically tense throughout the day and clenching your fists and mouth, for example, it is a deviation from the norm and your body is telling you something is wrong and feels bad. Unless you've just gone to the gym and you're noticing that you can't quite relax your muscles without paying attention to them, something is not ideal.

Focus ability. Ever have the feeling that you read a paragraph but realized you had no idea what it said so you had to go back and read it three more times? This is what the ability to focus is. When you can focus, your mind is fresh, you have energy, and you are excited for what's in front of you. When you don't have focus, your mind is murky, your eyes are glazed over, and you dread the thought of anything besides climbing into bed.

Compound this with not sleeping much and feeling muscle tightness all day and guess what—your body is telling you something. Unfortunately, the majority of us don't take hints until all of these signs strike together.

This is not something you can simply grind through. The changes you are implementing are too fast, too much, or too difficult. Take it down a notch.

For example, you might recognize in work situations that your muscles contract and tense up when you're faced with initiating a task or when you hear negative criticism from a superior. Once you identify this as a pattern, you can take steps to relieve yourself during the course of a workday—taking a walk, stretching, or having a snack with food or drink that are known for restoring or rejuvenating the physical areas you're feeling the most.

When you're more aware of how your body is operating, it's easier to assess whether changes in your course of action affect you, especially if the actions you take are proving to be injurious, stressful, or harmful. As you move forward, you can develop methods and techniques—such as deep breathing, muscle relaxation, yoga, or meditation—that can help you control your stress levels.

Monitoring Your Behavior

Self-awareness is a tricky topic. We regard many successful people as those who dismiss or disregard introspection as a hindrance to accomplishment or perceive analysis as an invitation to weakness. Steve Jobs is a frequent example—a genius so far ahead of his time in some ways that to doubt himself may legitimately have harmed his performance.

But not all of us are Steve Jobs—we need to monitor and track our own behaviors if we are to be at our most effective, and this is especially true if we are striving toward a goal. You might not even be able to know if you've reached your goal if you don't keep track.

Tracking our behavior is *not* the same as tracking our thoughts. In behavior change, our thoughts and motivations aren't significant. One could argue that our personal value is tied to more than just how we act or what we achieve—but those actions and achievements are all people can see of us and what they're more likely to be concerned about. Intentions and thoughts are unimportant to the bottom line of creating a change. Actions really do speak louder than words.

Through monitoring behavior independently of opinions, views, and intentions, that behavior will become the indicators of who we really are. This behavior will represent our objectives to the rest of the world and how we'll follow our goals through to completion.

Science backs up the fact that keeping watch on our conduct actually helps us create true change, through an occurrence known as *self-monitoring reactivity* (William J. Fremouw & John P. Brown Jr., 1980). This is simply when we begin to change *because* we monitor, measure, and report our results.

Self-monitoring works with both behaviors we want to increase and ones we want to decrease:

- Improving work focus, keeping on-task, and completing jobs
- Providing positive statements to peers
- Following instructions from teachers
- Reading text during study periods

When we know we're keeping track, we do it more (or less). There's no other way to know our behavior patterns, whether we're repeating them or trying to change them for the better. It's best to establish a baseline for at least one week and then fully document new behaviors day in and day out. How you log your behavior is up to you, whether it's with a checklist, ratings, stars, smiley faces—whatever's best for tracking your outcome, positive or negative.

Self-monitoring is nothing without self-honesty. It's absolutely necessary to ask yourself the difficult questions and provide sincere answers. Although it's tough to keep your mental defense mechanisms from intervening, try to subdue your thoughts, opinions, and intentions—focus squarely on your actions and nothing else. Try to keep it black and white, yes or no.

For example, say you're taking a certain subject in school or building knowledge of a topic for work, for which you have no fondness or think is prohibitively hard for you to learn.

You could start by initiating a daily checklist that covers your workspace, checking off when you've cleared the space of high-distraction items, turned off your smartphone, arranged your writing or note-taking needs like paper and pens. You could track how many pages you've read, how many notes you've taken, and how many minutes you've spent in active study.

These might seem like mundane things to keep close track of on a daily basis, but that's the point: by keeping track of the miniature behaviors that go along with preparing and executing your efforts, you're laying a mental groundwork for a routine to become part of a wider behavioral change. As such, no element is so minor that it shouldn't be included.

There are many methods and challenges that go along with self-monitoring behavior that are valuable to consider.

Expectations. Think about your current behaviors and expectations, then write down three separate lists:

- What you are doing
- What others think you should be doing
- What you believe you should be doing

Analyze these three lists side by side—in doing so, you'll find the gaps you should be fixing. Others may be wrong about you occasionally, but if you find that these lists keep disagreeing with each other (in essence, you are inconsistent with yourself and others), then you know there is a problem.

For example, if you've hit a wall with a writing project, stand back and analyze how you're currently going about it: researching on the web, taking notes, writing in spurts, perhaps missing deadlines.

Then list out what others believe (whether they've said so or not) you should be doing. This could be committing to a daily writing schedule, conducting personal interviews, sticking to deadlines, and planning how to publish your writing.

Finally, with those two columns complete, ask yourself what you personally believe you should be doing: confirming your sources, rewriting and polishing, being reasonable about what you can provide and when, and searching for publication routes once you're done. It's fine if some of the items on this list overlap with what others think you need to be doing.

This exercise helps to clear some of the conflicts you might be having by understanding your process and comparing expectations from the outside world and yourself. From this overhead view, you can get a better sense of what's most important and what you need to adapt.

Get objective feedback on your behavior from others. It's easy to understand how your own thoughts and beliefs might divert from or obscure your own analyses—so it's a perfectly acceptable idea to have someone else evaluate your behavior.

For example, if you've been working on a collaborative project at work, ask a trusted colleague for a frank discussion after it's reached a stopping point. Make sure they're clear that you just want to know about how they perceived your *behavior*, as opposed to your statements or your qualifications. Were your efforts consistent? How did you act as a conduit or a sounding board? What hours did you work? How did you bounce back from downtime? If there is a criticism, can you defend yourself based only on your actions, or do you have to refer to something like "I *meant* to, but..." Remember, actions speak louder than words.

Our keenest and starkest insights usually come when we realize and accept the viewpoints of others watching what we're doing. They can point out traits or behaviors we were completely unaware of and can address from a fresh vantage point. Do you need to do what you're doing more or less?

Limit your scope. We've thrown you a lot of information and options in this chapter. But once you've decided on a course of self-examination, try to identify a few key areas and maintain strict focus on them:

- **"What behaviors am I changing *from*?"** What past behaviors are you trying to evolve from or eliminate? Track this progress.

- **"What behaviors am I changing *to*?"** What new behaviors do you want to emulate and start doing? Track *this* progress.

- **"Why am I taking this course of action—what's in it for me?"** How will you benefit from this change, both short- and long-term? Track this progress, too.

- **"How am I going to make this work?"** Keeping in mind that short, simple strategies work the best, what's your game plan? Track this of course.

There's plenty of information you can use to assess how you're changing—but too much of it might hinder rather than help your goal. You might want to focus on only one or two of these metrics to guide your decisions.

Pivoting

You may come to the conclusion that, after self-monitoring your behavior or getting frustrated at how little you've progressed, a change in direction is in order.

Admitting that you've made mistakes is a positive step, it but requires you to make the difficult, frequently conscious choice to rein in your ego—that part of your mind that insists that you're never wrong or at fault. You have to kick the ego out of this process because, realistically, we're all wrong at various points in our lives. You need the humility to see where you've gone wrong or shown your faults. It's not self-deprecation or self-hating—it's an admirable honesty that will help spur your change in behavior. Accomplishing a goal isn't about being right!

Our ego's tendency to deflect blame can have several detrimental results. Consider the restaurant owner who shuts out feedback from his employees on how he's treating them or flaws he's making in restaurant operations. His ego tells him he's right and infallible. His inability to handle criticism causes him to set aside their suggestions and recommendations, creating a domino effect of low morale that could make the situation infinitely worse. Once Yelp reviewers get ahold of the conflict, it could be all over for

JJ's Waffles. Is it too late to hear the feedback and pivot?

To successfully pivot, you need thorough knowledge about what caused your failure, shortcoming, or lack of results. You have to get clear on the *individual* factors that caused the behavioral failures. It's vital to be accurate in attributing what causes the flaw—remember the adage *correlation does not mean causation*. You need to test your results to pinpoint the appropriate elements and change the right actions. Ideally you would be able to come up with a list of potential problems and go from there.

For example, let's say our ego-driven restaurant owner blames his falling fortunes on his staff's lack of enthusiasm or salesmanship. But that's nowhere nearly as important as the fact that his restaurant's fallen short at health inspections, that his recipes aren't what diners want, or that he's overcharging (or undercharging) for his food. Realizing the error of his ways, the owner can make decisions on rectifying those specific flaws. He's objectively examined his conclusions and applied them toward his overall aims. Good for him. But if he isn't able to figure out which is which, he's going to either be paralyzed or take the wrong path.

Pivoting also requires a sense of flexibility and not being wed to a certain method. This is also frequently due to ego, but sometimes habits, stubbornness, and fear play a role in an unwillingness to change. There's nothing wrong with going down the wrong road, as long as you turn back and find the right one. Understand, also, that perspective is an important quality that you can't gain without hitting one into the sand. A pivot is one of the best learning opportunities because it gives you an exponential amount of information versus when you only find success. With success, you learn that one potential path can work. With a failure and subsequent pivot, you learn that one potential path has any number of flaws, and your plan will be more fine-tuned than before.

Finally, pivoting is best when you know you want to achieve, because that will influence everything your new plan will require. The one thing that may remain after you blow everything up is the end point—your end goal. You may even have gotten distracted or been unable to see the forest for the trees.

Or it may be completely off-base and you may need to rethink everything you want. Sometimes drastic change is necessary, and you might not know it until you've started on the path already. When you pivot, it's critical to understand if your end goal is the same or has shifted. Only then can you see the path to making a lasting change.

Negative feedback, constructive criticism, and forced changes in direction are all too often seen as signs of failure in our overreactive world. That's fatalistic and frankly dangerous thinking. We may not always react happily to those situations, but we can't treat them as steps toward imminent collapse. Viewing and reviewing our actions in the course of change should be as fair and objective as we can manage. The agents of change are not the enemies—embrace them as strongly as you can.

Takeaways:

- When you get far enough along in your changes, you may need to stop and evaluate. In fact, you should, because things always look different when planning versus doing. So what needs to change in order for you to get back on track or optimize your progress?
- The first method of correcting course is to learn basic biofeedback. This is, in other words, how to listen to your body. If your body doesn't show any of the multiple signs of cumulative stress or anxiety, then you're on the right track. However, if your body is showing deviations in heart rate, energy, sleep, fatigue, and the ability to focus, you are acting in a counterproductive way and something needs to change.
- The second method of correcting course is to monitor and track your behavior meticulously. Only tracking behaviors (and not thoughts) can shed light on what you are doing on a daily basis, but it only works in conjunction with brutal honesty.

It is also important to understand your expectations and compare them with only your actions, solicit objective feedback from third parties, and understand exactly what you should track.

- If you've come to the point where you need to make a change, you must approach it with hat in hand and devoid of ego. You must not confuse correlation with causation, keep flexibility in mind, and remember what your end goal originally was and how it may have changed.

Chapter 7. Environment

The biggest obstacle we face in changing our behaviors could very well be one we might think we have no way to control: our environment. It's a factor that's often overlooked or understated, but it can be the most potent force of help or the most lethal force of damage.

An environment can be the deciding element of whether something is possible, hopeless, or unavoidable. If you wanted to become a great piano player, how might your environment factor into your improvement?

For instance, what if you lived in a piano warehouse? What if you didn't have a piano within driving distance? These are ways your environment can simply make something possible or impossible.

Supportive environments reinforce positive behaviors and cater to those who adhere to good practices. But unhelpful environments can produce fatigue and despondency in people who must fight to flourish. An inferior environment is often the real cause of problems that some might attribute to failures of will, discipline, or determination. Understandably, our internal motivation and willpower might take a back seat to what is dangling in our faces each day.

There's no better example of the contributions of an environment than the classroom. Endless studies (Dorman, Aldridge, & Fraser, 2006; Bucholz & Sheffler, 2009) cite how supportive classrooms where trust, encouragement, and free inquiry reign produce better outcomes and test scores than ones with little or no resources, low teacher morale, and lack of support.

German-American psychologist Kurt Lewin, one of the architects of social psychology, created a theoretical formula that is one of the most famous in the field: $B = f(P,E)$. Lewin's equation simply asserts that behavior (B) is a function (f) of a person (P) within their environment (E). Behavior is a combination of a person's unique attributes, combined with mitigating or encouraging factors in the person's most common physical surroundings. Lewin's dictum flew in the face of commonly accepted theories that claimed a person's *past* was the decisive element of their behavior (Ahem, Freud); he believed that the person's placement in a *current* situation fueled his or her conduct. This is more likely to be true for daily actions and habits, though not necessarily with underlying attachments and emotions.

Environment can, of course, be divided into two entities: physical and social. Physical environmental factors, of course, include everything in a given space that one can perceive with the five senses—sound, cleanliness, darkness, or light. As it relates to changing your behavior, this could be something that is physically unavoidable or completely absent—*out of sight, out of mind*. Social factors include everything from the people you surround yourself with, customs, and traditions to communication style, support models, and behavior.

Because an environment is usually perceived as a larger situation someone enters into, one might believe it's impossible to change the factors within that environment or to change the environment itself. But that's not true. It's entirely achievable to alter and manipulate your physical surroundings and interpersonal relations and to create situations that encourage your success.

Improve Your Environment

Adjusting your environment can make changing your behavior a whole lot easier. A new setting can help you bounce back from fixed ways of thinking you were unaware of and open up completely new avenues that can restore your enthusiasm and stimulate your effort.

This notion may seem disempowering. We'd prefer to think of success as the result of our own hard work—resolve, effort, and determination. Conversely, we fault failure on deficiencies in willpower, ability, talent, or performance. And for sure, all these personal factors count very highly in our accomplishments (or lack thereof).

But when you study how human behavior evolves over a long time period, environment frequently plays more of a part in success than motivation or skill. Environment is the hidden force that guides human behavior. Yes, incentive, aptitude, and labor are important, but these traits often get overmatched by the surroundings in which we dwell.

Habits and behavior argue for the "nurture" end of the "nature-or-nurture" debate—as does environment. External factors are the invisible accomplices for shaping how we react and behave. Over time, the environment conditions our actions and practices on a greater scale than our "natures"—our talents and beliefs—do. And it's possible to tweak those surroundings so we're enabled to use our talents, decision-making skills, and efforts in the most productive way possible.

Design Your Environment for Good Decisions

Brian Wansink of Cornell University conducted a study on dietary habits in 2006 and made an interesting discovery. When people switched from serving plates 12 inches in diameter to plates that were 10 inches, they wound up eating 22% *less* food. This finding was so effective that food writers have recycled it as a tip for diet success, to the extent that some espouse using tiny plates and tiny portions to curb appetites.

It's a great example of how even a minor adjustment in an environment can contribute to improved decision-making. The change in plate size was a minuscule two inches—not quite the width of a smartphone—but yielded more than one-fifth of a decrease in consumption. Repeated over time, this minor modification can build up good habits to make major impacts.

This practice is far more adaptable and versatile than you might think. The guiding principle is to make your environment more likely to trigger good habits you want to increase and hinder bad habits you want to eliminate—and making sure these triggers fit in the flow of your life.

If you want more incentive to practice a musical instrument more, for example, you could make a permanent place for the instrument in the middle of a room with instructions of exactly where to pick up. You could also leave a trail of sheet music that literally requires you to pick it up to walk to your bed. If you want to work out more, you're more likely to visit a gym if it's located on your way home from work, rather than 10 miles in the opposite direction.

You can also put your gym bag in front of your front door, buy a pull-up bar for your kitchen doorway, and only wear shoes that can double as exercise shoes. Finally, if you want to procrastinate less, you can leave reminder Post-its next to door handles and your wallet (things you will have to touch), leave your work in a place you can't avoid it, and hide your distracting temptations.

Decreasing bad habits is a function of *out of sight, out of mind*. For example, supermarkets often place higher-priced items at customers' eye levels to increase the chances they'll buy them. But one could *reverse* this process at home by keeping unhealthy foods away from immediate view and storing them in less visible or harder-to-reach levels. Put your chocolate inside five containers like a Russian nesting doll and put them in a closet—see how often you binge then.

To stop smoking, one might consider removing all the ashtrays from inside the home and place them as far away as possible on the perimeter of their property so smoking will necessitate a brisk walk in the freezing winter. To keep from sitting down all day, you can switch to a standing desk that will force you to stand up during most working hours. You could also simply remove chairs and coffee tables from the area in which you do most of your work.

The whole idea is to eliminate having to make decisions, because that's where we usually hit a snag. Depending on willpower and discipline is risky to say the least, so create an environment that will help you automate your decisions and make good habits the default choice. In taking that decision out of your hands, you're rewiring yourself to take bad habits out of your routine—and likely saving a little time in the process.

Author Mihaly Csikszentmihalyi, known for the book *Flow*, calls this general approach for changing environment changing one's *activation energy*—the less activation energy required to make good decisions and form good habits, the better. And by contrast, the higher the activation energy for completing a bad habit, the better. Activation energy can also be seen as the overall amount of effort people are willing to spend. By making the conscious choice to make harder activities more immediately accessible, they stand better chances of becoming permanent lifestyle changes.

Improving Your Social Support

Setting up your physical environment is a major step and at least somewhat easy to picture—more piano sheet music, less chocolate, more reminders, and fewer distractions. But if you don't have a solid social structure that reinforces your good habits, you're in danger of faltering every time you step out of your environment. That's the negative on manipulating your physical environment—it only works when you're *in* it. Social support, however, is with us day and night.

A recent study by the *New England Journal of Medicine* closely analyzed a social network consisting of 12,067 people. They had been monitored for 32 years between 1971 and 2003. Investigators had detailed information on the connections: who were friends, who were spouses, siblings, neighbors, and so forth. They also tracked how much each person in the network weighed at specific times over those three decades.

They found that members of this network tended to gain weight when their friends did, increasing their chances of obesity by 57%.

This wasn't the case when family members' weights changed; mainly friends and the people they interacted with the most. Whether these friends were located close by or across the country, they maintained the same influence. Very close friends were even likelier to gain weight—if one part of a pair of friends became obese, the other one's chances of becoming obese increased by a whopping 171%.

Whether they think they do or not, those around us have a huge influence on our lives. They can support us, discourage us, or remain wholly apathetic to our goals. Any of these can have a lasting effect on whether we are able to reach our definition of success. For instance, say you wanted to learn piano, but three of your close friends announced that piano was for *nerds* and *losers*. How likely is it that you will persist in this goal, knowing the social pressures and stigmas associated with it? We tend to take others' behaviors around us somewhat personally, as a reflection of our friendship.

But like our physical environment, we can change our social environments as well.

When it comes to others' negativism or indifference, it's more about *them*, not us. If they express negativity about what you want, it's probably because they're envious or resentful that they don't have the courage to do what you're doing. If you're nervous and excited about a new job that answers to your interests, they might deflate your excitement because they're stuck in their own rut. If you're excited about buying your first house, they may bring you down by making disparaging judgments about the neighborhood you're moving to—just because they can't afford to buy a house themselves.

If they're apathetic, that's just a reflection that you're not the main concern in their life. Which is fine—you don't have to be. Your friends may not be as excited as you are about finding a new personal trainer or taking a class to expand your skills, because it's not something terribly important to them. In return, they may not expect you to be over-excited about their new diet or music appreciation class.

None of these attitudes in and of themselves are reasons to end a friendship—but it's possible to surround yourself with a social framework that's more supportive of your needs—and at least cares enough to throw you an encouraging word and ask about your progress occasionally. We can't choose who our families are, but we can adjust our friendship circles to be conducive to our goals.

We can keep an eye out for social members who can fill specific roles in our support environment.

Accountability partner. This is a person who shares your successes, acts as a motivator, and keep you on course. This is someone you report (daily, weekly, monthly) to so you can make sure you're doing what you should be doing, and they do the same. You share each other's challenges, concerns, and victories, and you regenerate each other through work challenges, family situations, health issues, daily practical matters, ambitions, and goals.

They're also a sounding board of ideas and experience, as you are with them. The chances for mutual growth with an accountability partner are excellent.

Mentors, role models, and teachers. There are likely at least one or two people we hold up as examples of who we'd like to be. While this kind of admiration shouldn't translate into meaningless hero worship, there's good reason to spend as much time as you can with them to see their habits in action. Observe their best practices and mindsets, and practice emulating them to see how it affects your behavior. Even seek to connect with them and seek direct guidance.

Of course, there's a chance that they may not be everything you thought they are—which is fine. They don't have to be superheroes, and seeing them as normal people might make your journey more navigable and approachable. Just keep in mind that you can learn from them in a few specific ways, so pay attention.

New people. An interesting theory is that you're the average of the five people you spend the most time with. They could be all the same kind of people or wildly different from each other, but they have significant influence on your thoughts and deeds. The implication is that we are truly products of our social environments, and we pick up an immeasurable number of thoughts just being in the presence of people.

Is that positive or negative? That's what you have to find out. You never want to be the most superlative positive member—the "smartest," the "prettiest," the "richest"—of any given group—because that means the averages of the other people are dragging you down. This isn't meant to sound judgmental or catty; it's just that if you truly want to prioritize achieving your goals and expanding in substantial ways, you may need to find another group to spend time with. Surround yourself with better piano players, smarter businesspeople, or more disciplined entrepreneurs.

This is an inherently uncomfortable process because it likely involves you seeking out intimidating people and the realization that you are now a small fish in a large pond. But it's part of the process of moving onward and upward. Don't abandon your friends, your social network, or your groups; just understand the power of the people around you.

Keep yourself low-maintenance. There's as much value—more, potentially—in receiving passive support from your network, so let them know they don't have to exert too much effort beyond consistent emotional support. There's really nothing much to that kind of support at all; it's relatively easy to dispense and doesn't wear others out. Just let them know they're important to you and that you value them whether they're in your everyday existence or if they're further away. The residual support may be enough to get you through without their lifting a finger.

The task of altering our environments shouldn't be as onerous as it looks on paper. Most of the effort consists of small but meaningful adjustments that change the flow around you, just enough to start new patterns and change your behavior for the better.

Takeaways:

- The environments we find ourselves in have a startling ability to influence whether or not we reach our goals. Environments can be encouraging or discouraging, or they make matters flat out possible or impossible.
- Environment can be split into the physical environment and social environment. Both matter, though physical can be said to be restrained to when you are *in* it.
- To manipulate your physical environment for greater success, you want to make it easier and to take less *activation energy* to complete good habits while making it more difficult for bad habits to persist. This is for the purpose of making good decisions your easiest default action.

- Manipulating your social environment is more difficult but possibly more effective because it stays with you day and night. You are the average of the five people you spend the most time with, so you can look into finding an accountability partner, mentors, role models, and overall new people.

Chapter 8. Building Lasting Habits

Behavioral change doesn't happen overnight, of course. It's a deliberate act that requires conscious attention. Habits, on the other hand, are involuntary. We don't even think about them; they're innate parts of our nature.

Even though they're opposites, the goal of changing our behaviors is to create habits. Though the process of behavioral change can be long and extended, possibly frustrating at some points, the desired result is to create a slate of routines that we don't have to think about and rather just *happen*.

The brain isn't stagnant—it changes and develops well into adulthood. It constantly reconstructs itself for the entire duration of a human life, both in substance and utility. The stimuli for this perpetual evolution is what happens in your surroundings, actions, reasoning, and feelings. This persistent activity the brain undergoes is generally referred to as *neuroplasticity*.

The idea of neuroplasticity is not a recent development. As far back as the 19th century, scientists have theorized about the brain's elasticity, viewing it as a growing and changing organism within an organism. This perception superseded the previously understood opinion that the adult brain was stagnant after a certain point, that it solidified itself after certain crucial formative phases in childhood. While it's true that the brain is more flexible during its early years and that its abilities decrease as we grow older, its plasticity and flexibility remain in effect throughout its lifespan.

Recent developments in technology—specifically, functional magnetic resonance imaging (fMRI)—now allow us to observe the brain's malleable nature and its remarkable ability to alter itself as we grow, experience, and mature. This relatively new kind of visualization has confirmed what we have long theorized: the brain is a morphing machine that never stops processing and adapting. As such, habits are a matter of brain chemistry that we can transform.

Forming Habits Takes Time

In the words of Aristotle, "Good habits formed at youth make all the difference." Building habits is thought to be easier in youth because our minds are more malleable, but altering habits is possible regardless of age.

Phillippa Lally, a health psychology researcher at University College London, published a study in the *European Journal of Social Psychology* that aimed to find out just how long the process of habit formation really takes. The study was conducted over the course of 12 weeks and examined the behavior of 96 participants who chose habits that they would try to build and then reported daily on how automatic the behavior felt. After analyzing the data, Lally and her team determined that, on average, it took 66 days for a daily action to become automatic.

How long it takes you to develop a new habit will depend on your existing habits and behavior as well as your personal circumstances. The quickest habit in Lally's study was developed in only 18 days, while the slowest took 254 days.

Positive habits are crucial to accomplishing behavior change because once you have a habit, it's second nature. You can think of good habits like frozen, automatic self-discipline that guides you to where you want to go in life. They are your subconscious, automatic response that doesn't require extra effort on your part.

Something that initially requires a lot of self-discipline, for example, is daily exercise. So to build that habit, you might schedule it at the same time every day and then give yourself a little reward immediately afterward to incentivize yourself to do it. After a month (or two months, as Lally's study found), you won't even need much self-discipline anymore, so long as you stick to your habits.

The lesson here is straightforward. Building habits takes time, and it requires self-discipline to get through that process. But once you make it through that phase, your habit will drive you to achieve where you used to require exercising self-discipline. Expect that you will require at least two months and settle in for the long haul.

It will take quite a while for the annoyance and discomfort of forming habits to vanish. You might still feel them on rare occasions, but having already built the habit will make it much easier to control whatever negative urges do arise.

First, avoid self-sabotage. That means that you want to start small and manageable with habits rather than shooting for the stars right away and guaranteeing failure. If you're out of shape and want to get fit, start with taking a 20-minute walk every day rather than immediately jumping into a workout routine that will make you sore and miserable. Twenty minutes of walking is such an attainable goal that it's impossible to come up with an excuse not to do it. Start with five minutes if you need to pare it down.

Starting small reduces the perceived difficulty of the task and will make it easier to stick with it when your motivation is lacking. It tells your brain that this action is acceptable and even enjoyable. It also builds a level of anticipation and expectation for the action. And of course, you can steadily increase the duration or difficulty of your new habit as you feel yourself progressing.

Whenever you do feel highly motivated in the initial stages of habit formation, you can certainly take advantage of that to make bigger strides toward your goal. But keep in mind that being disciplined and putting in the effort will not always feel exhilarating. And if you can't do it when it feels bad or you feel annoyed, the habit isn't going to stick. So savor the motivation when you have it, but don't get addicted to that feeling.

Some days will be easy and you'll use positive emotions to overachieve. There will also be plenty of times when emotion runs low and you really have to tap into your willpower and self-discipline to fulfill the habit formation process. But if you persevere for long enough, the rollercoaster ride eventually comes to a halt and your new behavior becomes a habit and a permanent part of your life. Tasks that once required mental fortitude will become as easy and natural as breathing.

Know Your Triggers

Changing behavior is a thought-intensive process, and it requires us to get to the heart of why we act the way we do. What leads us to act out our bad habits? What stops us from picking up good ones?

Answering this question helps learn the crux of our behavioral challenges by revealing what triggers our actions. These triggers are what we need to zero in on.

Once we discover what the triggers for our habits are, according to neuroscientists, we can start trying to reverse what they produce. It's possible for one to "rewire" the neurological avenues by very deliberately exchanging the bad habits being triggered with beneficial ones.

To start, make a close observation at the situations that might provoke you into executing a bad habit. For example, writer Philip Galanes supposed that your desire to be a control freak over other people's lives might be manifesting in your setting hard times for meetings that are convenient for you, not them.

Another possibility is what psychological professionals term "neurotic behavior": the acts that come from a self-destructive desire to destroy ourselves. One might block or try to derail success because they don't think they deserve to have a good life. Or one might resist taking up good health habits because our body doesn't deserve to feel well. An addict may be driven by an inner need to diminish or terminate their life. These suspect, hard-to-detect impulses get entangled with the effects we've enacted through events in our lives.

There's also the matter of reinforcements, the rewards that bolster our behaviors. It's impossible not to respond to reinforcements. Certain bad habits keep getting repeated because they feel good. They also might help temporarily relieve stress, which becomes *another* reinforcement. As long as a bad habit subtracts discomfort and adds pleasure on a surface level, it can be hard to understand why it has to go.

Our social existences in society also inform our habits. If nobody complains about your chronic lateness, your domineering manner, or your intense social awkwardness, you might not see any cause for changing. And *other* people's bad behavior could encourage yours. You might be late to an important meeting, which forces everyone who got there on time to fill you in on what you've missed. Your dramatic entrance has made everyone give you their attention and concern. Mission accomplished. (Or is that submission?)

If you can determine the root cause of an adverse habit, you can also try to change the *consequences* of your behavior. If a certain bad habit gives you pleasure, attention from others, or some kind of thrill, try to allow yourself those minor joys as rewards for *positive* behavior.

If getting attention for your blunders or lateness is something that reinforces you, try some other avenue to get that attention: write a thoughtful blog post and publish it on social media, or take a couple of hours to volunteer in a group setting. If overusing alcohol alleviates your stress, trying to switch it out with herbal tea or aromatherapy. If you just can't give up the taste of a hamburger for the sake of health, find a recipe for a black bean burger that will satisfy your taste requirements.

It might take a little elbow grease to devise ways to replace the false satisfaction we get from bad habits—but it's entirely practical and intensely beneficial to do so. And it might not be as much of an effort as you're inclined to believe, especially when you start feeling better on a genuine, real level.

The If-Then Technique

This method is a surefire way to work with the disarray, confusion, and disorder life presents you and to stick to your intentions no matter what's thrown at you. It's also extremely simple. While considering your desired change, simply replace the italics in this phrase: "If *something unexpected*, then *your response*."

Complete these phrases *before* you are in a dire situation and you can see how they work for you. It is like creating a rule for yourself to abide by. If you've given it thought beforehand, you can default to that guideline and not have to try to make a risky decision in the heat of the moment. Anticipate what's to happen and you are a step ahead of the game.

For example, it's your birthday, but you're on a strict diet and your office has a thing for surprise parties so you'll probably be getting one. "If they brought cake, then I'll get a small slice or take it home and casually forget to eat it." Alternately, you could be having a problem with procrastination, and you're settling in for a big project you have to finish. You could say, "If the phone rings, then I'll ignore it until I'm done or only answer if it's a family member and then keep it brief," or "If I get a news alert, then I'll only look at it quickly and not visit a news website."

You could obviously get more detailed with these statements and can prepare them for situations with more significance or danger than the above examples. But whatever the case, the if-then method forces you to project yourself into common scenarios that could trigger reversion to your bad habits—and makes you plan for those triggers. It takes away your residuals of false justification and excuses for doing the wrong thing (or doing nothing) and sharpens your commitment to meeting your goals.

All of these methods help focus on the minute but powerful triggers that lead us into the personal infractions we're trying to eliminate, and they help defray the residual personal reactions that arise from forcing change in our lives. Best of all, they don't rely on sweeping or exhaustive changes to who we are—they make our brains and natural impulses work *for* us instead of going to sleep on the job.

Takeaways:

- Building habits, though it appears to be contrary to behavior change, is actually the end goal we are shooting for. We want our new actions and behaviors to be automatic, and research has indicated that it takes around two months to actually create a habit to the point where it is an instinctual, subconscious action. This means consistency is important, no matter how small it is.

- A large part of habits is finding the triggers that either keep you on track or hold you back.
- The if-then technique allows you to set guidelines and anticipate the hardships you may face. If you face a future situation, then you will already have a prescribed reaction. In this way, you can avoid using willpower and discipline and react with your rule.

Chapter 9. Design Flaws

We've delved into what propels behavior change: why people act in the ways that they do. We've examined how we can control our brain chemistry and psychology and exploit them for our improvement. Even with all this new and powerful knowledge, there are strategic pitfalls that could arise. If you've come up with a faulty or ineffective plan focused on the wrong habits or made a strategic error, you might not make the changes you're seeking.

That's why this chapter takes a look at some common design flaws that can derail your efforts in changing behavior—or keep you on the same, unchanged track on which change never happens.

B.J. Fogg's Mistakes for Change

We mentioned B.J. Fogg and his concept of *tiny habits* back in Chapter 1. Fogg also identified some common mistakes in thinking, framing, and approach to behavior change that frequently happen—and how to adapt one's way of thinking to correct course and push change forward.

Relying on willpower for long-term change. Willpower, for all its merits, is a finite and inconstant resource. You can regenerate it, of course, but you can't rely on raw will to lead you through a protracted period of behavioral change. Trying to keep an exercise program, a diet, or system of work discipline going through sheer will alone could deplete the mental faculties that control will and lead to what scientists call "ego depletion."

Fogg's solution is to pretend that willpower isn't even an available option. Instead, narrow your focus on the smaller behavior changes that can lead to eventual development of larger-scale changes—build your new behavior brick by brick, from the ground up. This is why environments are so important to manipulate.

Attempting big leaps instead of baby steps. We tend to focus on change as an overwhelming, major event—not a series of smaller steps that lead practically to a positive solution. We celebrate when a baseball team wins the World Series, not when they win the first game of spring training.

That view undermines the truth that it takes a lot of smaller work for change to be successful, and it can distort our strategy. We feel underwhelmed when we've lost only one pound over the course of a week or when we don't have complete knowledge of a school subject after reading the material only once. This could lead us to overshoot our ambitions too early and attempt to crank major efforts out in less time than anyone possibly can.

Again, Fogg urges us to focus on the smaller picture and celebrate the miniature progress we make step by step. Realizing the larger goal is fine, but building new behaviors relies on the accumulation of smaller but still significant victories. Everything starts with something small, and sometimes it's hard to see how it can contribute to the end goal—but they can and do.

Trying to stop old behaviors instead of creating new ones. Successfully stopping a bad habit by going "cold turkey" is more the exception than the rule. We make vows to stop smoking or drinking by shutting consumption down completely. But this frequently fails because we haven't come up with an answer for the cravings we feel; we've just told ourselves we're going to deal with the discomfort without knowing how. Your brain is still expecting to be satisfied with the behavior you're cutting off, and your brain is not happy about this.

The solution is to replace the old behavior or routine with a new one—but one that delivers some kind of compensatory reward that the brain can understand. If you're trying to give up sugary sweets but your brain craves the reward, try eating a piece of healthy fruit. If you're craving a cigarette, try finding a motor activity—playing piano, housecleaning, or building furniture—that gives you a sense of accomplishment. Simply telling someone to stop indulging is tough; replacing that feeling is both more productive and sustainable.

Believing that information leads to action. I really hope you've enjoyed this book and that it gave you a lot of valuable information. But you're not done, even though this book nearly is.

Knowing the facts about a certain situation does not equal working on it. You can tell someone why it's important to stop smoking, exercise, or increase their attention span, but that's not sufficient stimuli in and of itself. Rationalization is almost always useless; there needs to be a motivating action as well.

Instead of gathering more intel on what you need to do, begin applying the information in real situations. Focus on identifying your triggers, adjusting your patterns, putting effort into it, and recording your results on a regular basis. As Mike Tyson once said, *"Everyone has a plan until they get punched in the face."* Your plans, based on all the information you've gathered, might be useless once you start and realize they won't work for you. Leap before you look occasionally.

Seeking to change a behavior forever, not for a short time. This is similar to the second of Fogg's flaws: trying to make huge changes instead of smaller ones. Instead of the *size* of the change, this failing concerns the *time* element. Making overly ambitious proclamations that we'll banish the bad and embrace the good until the end of time distorts the reality of change—again, that it's the culmination of several small changes executed faithfully over an extended period of time. This is why 12-step programs focus on the "now" and tracking progress "one day at a time."

The solution to this problem is at least a little obvious: limit the range of time you're focusing on and accept the accomplishment of changing on a smaller scale and a day-by-day frame of mind. Don't try to eat the whole pie at once because you'll defeat yourself mentally. Just take it one slice at a time, focus on the present, and see what you can do to keep moving forward. With behavior and habits, just focus on what you can do at the present moment.

James Clear's Mistakes That Cause New Habits to Fail

James Clear "studies successful people across a wide range of disciplines... to uncover the habits and routines that make these people the best at what they do." He shares his findings in a popular newsletter.

After a few years of careful inspection, Clear uncovered some typical mistakes that keep new habits from taking root in people trying to change their behavior. Clear and Fogg offer some similar perspectives on these mistakes, but Clear identifies two more common errors committed by those seeking to alter their behaviors and habits.

Seeking a result, not a ritual. We tend to value the *payoff* in contemporary society. We're looking to lose 100 pounds, increase our productivity by 110%, finish first in the marathon, and, if we have time, stave off death forever. We may value effort, but if it doesn't produce the results we want exactly as we want them, we consider that effort to have failed.

The problem with this, Clear says, is that "New goals don't deliver new results. New lifestyles do." For this reason, he suggests envisioning behavior change as something that happens every day—as a ritual.

Over time and repetition, these rituals add up and produce solid lifestyle changes. It may be frustrating that we don't see immediate effects from a day or two of changing behavior. But we can gauge progress more incrementally—after a year, a month, or even a week.

The trick is putting your thoughts, emotions, and efforts into keeping the ritual. Focus on the 15-minute jog, the 20 minutes of meditation, the 30 minutes of studying, or the hour of music practice that you repeat every day. You can refine or add to those rituals as you keep them up—but keep your mind oriented on the routine in and of itself.

Assuming small changes don't add up. In a similar vein, our focus on big payoffs often conjures up an idea of the minimum that we want to accomplish. In addition to the 100 pounds we want to lose, mentioned above, we want to successfully complete three semesters of five classes each, make $50,000 in commissions, and sew 100 uniforms for our children's high school marching band. With all these grand schemes, we tend to downgrade the asset of patience.

Clear says this leads us to believe that "achievements need to be big to make a difference." But again, in reality the habits we have today are the accrual of the good and bad options we've selected over years and years.

Like he suggests with developing rituals, Clear suggests centering on small changes and developing them over a series of time to enable wholesale habit changes down the road. "Build the behavior first," Clear says. "Worry about the results later."

Takeaways:

- The psychological design flaws we encounter in changing our behaviors take a few predictable forms.

- B.J. Fogg articulated a few: relying on willpower and discipline, shooting for big steps rather than small, trying to stop old behaviors rather than start new ones, believing that information leads to change, and trying to change a behavior forever rather than just for today.

- James Clear also articulated two design flaws in changing our behavior: seeking a result above all else and assuming small changes don't add up.

Summary Guide

Chapter 1. Models of Behavior Change

- Behavior change is not a new topic, as people have wanted to improve themselves for millennia. The more recent, historical models of behavior change inform the framework for what we use today.

- Historical models of behavior change include classical conditioning (unconscious association), operant conditioning (trained actions), tiny habits (taking baby steps, changing your context, or having an epiphany), and cognitive behavioral theory (fixing automatic thought patterns that are detrimental).

- The transtheoretical model of change is what parallels daily struggle the most thoroughly and is composed of six stages: precontemplation, contemplation, preparation, action, maintenance, and termination.

Chapter 2. What's Holding You Back?

- Even though we logically and intellectually know what we should do, why don't do we those things? Because despite what we like to think, we aren't really operating on conscious free will most of the time. There are three categories of obstacles to really doing what we want at any point: *conscious, subconscious,* and *external* factors.

- Conscious factors are ones we know and readily tell ourselves. They are what we repeat when we fail or decide not to do something. They include low self-esteem, negative self-image, over-tolerance with pain or discomfort, aversion to confrontation, and fear of failure and rejection.

- Subconscious factors are similar to the conscious factors, yet they are so deeply ingrained in our identities we don't even realize we hold these beliefs—they are just our automatic thought patterns. They include limiting beliefs and narratives, having a fixed mindset, and being victim to traumatic experiences.

- External factors are outside of ourselves. They are the environmental or social pressures that keep us from taking action. Some of these are legitimate; some are simply excuses. These include lack of knowledge, too many obligations, too comfortable, harmful environments, social inertia, or rejection.

Chapter 3. What's Pushing You Forward?

- Though motivations are important, motivations won't get you to your goals—they are short-term solutions to long-term

problems. An emphasis on motivation is an emphasis on unsustainable practices.
- The same three categories apply with motivations as with obstacles: conscious, subconscious, and external.
- Conscious motivations include our positive emotions and positioning ourselves to experience them, while subconscious motivations include compensating for insecurity and confirming your self-identity. External motivations are the ways we experience the world around us, from social relationships, to money, to power, to our surroundings.
- Finally, Maslow's hierarchy of needs represents a set of universal motivations that accurately portray why people are preoccupied or *stuck*. The stages of the hierarchy are physiological fulfillment, safety, love and belonging, self-esteem, and self-actualization. Many people will never make it through the entire hierarchy.

<u>Chapter 4. Start Your Engines</u>

- Getting started on changing your behavior is the most difficult part because it involves confronting fear, uncertainty, and making a leap of faith.

- Aside from the psychological reasons, you may also be unwittingly procrastinating. Perfectionism and over-planning are forms of covert procrastination because they allow us to keep spinning our wheels from the comfort of never starting. Beware that you are not using these as excuses to yourself.

- SMART goals are helpful in getting started because it is too easy to set goals that actually detract from your motivation. SMART goals consist of five aspects: specific, measurable, attainable, relevant, and time-bound.

- Seek to break your tasks into as small of tasks as possible in order to reduce intimidation and simply make it easy to do something—anything. Break boulders into pebbles and see that every boulder is simply composed of nearly weightless pebbles that you can move at a moment's notice. You can ask yourself any of the questions ("What can I Google right now?") to see the types of small tasks you can immediately engage in.

- Embrace the beginner's mindset, because it will help temper your expectations and keep you open-minded to the possibility of failure. Beginners often fail—why wouldn't they? It would be odd if they didn't. Therefore, if you don't expect to succeed linearly, getting started suddenly seems much easier.

Chapter 5. Maintain Momentum

- Momentum is what keeps us persisting toward our goals even in hard times. Yet, it is hard to find and easy to be knocked off of.

- Momentum is most likely when you can avoid burnout, feelings of pointlessness, and boredom by understanding the Yerkes-Dodson curve.

- Pacing is also important to sticking with your behavior changes, and it involves understanding Parkinson's law, taking *combinatory play* breaks, scheduling for failure, scheduling and prioritizing your practice, and occasionally riding yourself to the brink of exhaustion just because you're in the zone.

Chapter 6. Correcting Course

- When you get far enough along in your changes, you may need to stop and evaluate. In fact, you should, because things always look different when planning versus doing. So what needs to change in order for you to get back on track or optimize your progress?
- The first method of correcting course is to learn basic biofeedback. This is, in other words, how to listen to your body. If your body doesn't show any of the multiple signs of cumulative stress or anxiety, then you're on the right track. However, if your body is showing deviations in heart rate, energy, sleep, fatigue, and the ability to

focus, you are acting in a counterproductive way and something needs to change.
- The second method of correcting course is to monitor and track your behavior meticulously. Only tracking behaviors (and not thoughts) can shed light on what you are doing on a daily basis, but it only works in conjunction with brutal honesty. It is also important to understand your expectations and compare them with only your actions, solicit objective feedback from third parties, and understand exactly what you should track.
- If you've come to the point where you need to make a change, you must approach it with hat in hand and devoid of ego. You must not confuse correlation with causation, keep flexibility in mind, and remember what your end goal originally was and how it may have changed.

Chapter 7. Environment

- The environments we find ourselves in have a startling ability to influence whether or not we reach our goals. Environments can be encouraging or discouraging, or they make matters flat out possible or impossible.
- Environment can be split into the physical environment and social environment. Both matter, though physical can be said to be restrained to when you are *in* it.
- To manipulate your physical environment for greater success, you want to make it easier and to take less *activation energy* to complete good habits while making it more difficult for bad habits to persist. This is for the purpose of making good decisions your easiest default action.
- Manipulating your social environment is more difficult but possibly more effective because it stays with you day and night. You are the average of the five people you spend the most time with, so you can look into finding an accountability partner, mentors, role models, and overall new people.

Chapter 8. Building Lasting Habits

- Building habits, though it appears to be contrary to behavior change, is actually the end goal we are shooting for. We want our new actions and behaviors to be automatic, and research has indicated that it takes around two months to actually create a habit to the point where it is an instinctual, subconscious action. This means consistency is important, no matter how small it is.
- A large part of habits is finding the triggers that either keep you on track or hold you back.
- The if-then technique allows you to set guidelines and anticipate the hardships you may face. If you face a future situation, then you will already have a prescribed reaction. In this way, you can avoid using willpower and discipline and react with your rule.

Chapter 9. Design Flaws

- The psychological design flaws we encounter in changing our behaviors take a few predictable forms.

- B.J. Fogg articulated a few: relying on willpower and discipline, shooting for big steps rather than small, trying to stop old behaviors rather than start new ones, believing that information leads to change, and trying to change a behavior forever rather than just for today.

- James Clear also articulated two design flaws in changing our behavior: seeking a result above all else and assuming small changes don't add up.

Made in the USA
Lexington, KY
02 July 2019